Human Nature

Christopher J. Berry

HUMANITIES PRESS INTERNATIONAL, INC.
ATLANTIC HIGHLANDS, NJ

First published in 1986 in the United States of America by
HUMANITIES PRESS INTERNATIONAL, INC., Atlantic Highlands, NJ 07716

LIBRARY OF CONGRESS CATALOGING IN PUBLICATION DATA

Berry, Christopher J.
   Human nature.
   (Issues in political theory)
   Bibliography: p.
   1. Political science. 2. Man. 3. Natural law.
4. Social values. I. Title. II. Series.
JA74.B47   1986   320'.01'1   86-7190
ISBN 0-391-03434-0
ISBN 0-391-03433-2 (pbk.)

PRINTED IN HONG KONG

To Christine

Contents

Preface

The topic 'human nature and politics' can be approached in many different ways and raises a wide variety of issues. It follows from this that a book very different from the present one could have been relevantly written on the same topic. I cannot therefore hope to satisfy all the expectations that a book of this title might generate. Accordingly I wish initially to identify the task that I have set myself.

There are two negative points in this identification. First, I am not here dealing with narrowly analytical questions. Thus I will not be exploring issues like how a view of free-will relates to key problems in political theory such as punishment and merit. Neither am I engaged, as Hume said he was, in anatomising human nature. There are hence no discussions as such of reason or the emotions or imagination and how these affect the character and meaning of political life. Nor, unlike Derek Parfit (1984), am I a Theseus entering into the labyrinth of problems concerning the self and personal identity and the bearing these have on questions of responsibility, autonomy, rights and so on. Second, I am not here putting forward an interpretation as to what human nature *is*. I am not, in other words, legislating or advocating that a particular view of the structure or substance of human nature is the correct one.

The positive aim of this book is to focus on the 'work' that a concept of human nature does and how this work bears on politics. My guiding question is: what is the point of referring to or invoking human nature? This means that I am engaged in examining what is assumed or presupposed when the idea of human nature is invoked (even if this invocation is only implicit). That examination is the book's raison d'être.

The notion of human nature is both basic and elusive. We can see the political importance of the idea at two levels. Firstly, at the conceptual level, while 'human nature' is not obviously an 'issue'

like 'equality' or 'justice' or the other topics that will be dealt with in
this series it is implicit within them. Indeed it is not going too far to
say that conceptions of human nature are basic to making equality,
justice and the rest political 'issues' in the first place. Though basic
in this sense the concept is elusive in that it is scarcely ever examined
in its own right. This book aims to fill that 'gap'. If successful the
reason why human nature is basic will become apparent and the
concept's elusiveness will be diminished by having its basic
analytical structure identified.

Secondly, at a popular or informal level, the notion of human
nature is politically important because of both the frequency and
context of its use in everyday discourse. The frequency with which
'human nature' is invoked is indicated by the almost proverbial use
of the expressions 'that's human nature' and 'it's only human
nature'. The context in which these invocations are made is one
where explanation and justification are called for. The political
significance of this is that 'human nature' has a prominent place in
the repertoire of explanations and justifications that is embedded in
popular consciousness. It is this consciousness that is largely
responsible for the perceptions people have of their society and it is
these perceptions that directly affect their political beliefs and
actions. Accordingly, examination of the concept of human nature
is of more than a narrowly academic interest and should, if
successful, help throw light on the 'real world' of political
experience.

This popular usage of the idea of human nature distinguishes it
once more from the other staple ingredients of political theory
which generally betray a more deliberate or heightened self-
consciousness. That is not to say, of course, that thought about
human nature has not been couched in a reflective mode but the
general unreflectiveness that characterises its popular usage is part
and parcel of its political force. Let me give two connected
examples.

In the correspondence columns of *The Observer* (London), 31
July 1983, two letters were published on the theme of employment.
One correspondent remarked, 'Unemployment is not caused by
skills becoming obsolescent – human nature is too ingenious for that
to be a serious problem'; the other correspondent recommended
that 'we share out jobs in formal employment as generously as
human nature will permit'. What is significant here is, firstly, that

'human nature' is introduced into the discussion at all. It is likely that it was just assumed, without any great reflection, to be a relevant factor. But if we do reflect upon the 'work' that the notion is doing in these letters we can discern a basic structure to the concept of human nature.

The very introduction of 'human nature' indicates that the concept is seen as a factor that has to be taken into account when discussing social policy. In this sense, therefore, what is regarded as human nature has practical significance. Further analysis reveals that it is being assumed that it is not a matter of certain individuals being ingenious, but rather that this is a universal trait shared by all; everyone as a human being is able to acquire new skills. This ability is a given about Man, thus making it practical to consider investment in retraining schemes. However, according to the second correspondent, it is also a given that there are constraints on what can be actually achieved in the way of reform. Again it is not a question of just a few individuals being perhaps reluctant to share wholeheartedly but a characteristic possessed by all. Someone else, however, might contest this by saying that such reluctance would evaporate once the experience of sharing takes place because what is truly given about Man is communal fellow-feeling.

What do these letters tell us about the work done by the idea of human nature? I believe that they reveal that the concept of human nature possesses a basic structure that has three aspects or facets. On my interpretation the concept of human nature is (i) a practical concept, is (ii) used to point out universal features of human beings and (iii) serves to indicate what is given about humanity.

(i) When I claim that human nature is a practical concept I mean that the concept is invoked when considering human action, when considering what it is appropriate or suitable for humans to do. For example, as the above letters indicate, appeals to human nature are often made in the context of deciding what is the proper way to organise economic life. One such issue is whether or not incentives are necessary. Do differential rewards have to be offered so that certain jobs in society are undertaken? If it is assumed that humans would only do dangerous or unpleasant or responsible jobs if they were given a reward greater than those who do not undertake those occupations then it is being assumed that for humans work is a 'cost'. Work is an instrumental activity done for the sake of something other than itself. On this assumption incentives are

xii   *Preface*

necessary. Conversely, if it is assumed that it is human nature to engage in meaningful activity, to express one's character and to stamp one's identity onto the world, then work is not a cost but an activity undertaken for its own sake. The relevance of this to politics should now be apparent. Starting from the latter assumption the reason why incentives seem to be needed is because work, as currently organised, has no meaning. It is because work is tedious, repetitive, trivial and unimaginative that leisure and repose are valued instead. Since economic organisation is a practical matter, is something within the scope of human action, then working practices should be changed. Yet if it is assumed work is a cost and it is human nature to prefer repose there is no need to apologise for differentials since they fit the structure of human nature.

(ii) When I claim that universality is a facet of human nature I mean that when the concept is invoked it is being asserted that what is attributed to human nature is true for all humans. We can illustrate the force of this from the example just given. The argument for incentives claimed that it is human nature to prefer repose to work. Because this is a claim about human nature then it is also being claimed that the need for incentives is not the product of a particular social order. Accordingly it applies as equally to the inhabitants of the Kalihari desert, who bestir themselves to locate the grubs that form a staple part of their diet, as it does to workers in a complex industrial society who labour for money to buy the goods they need and want. The same claims to universality are implicit in the view that it is human nature to engage in meaningful activity hence, it could be argued, the ubiquity of art and ritual in all cultures.

(iii) When I claim that givenness is a facet of human nature I mean that when the concept is invoked certain constraints upon human beings are also being invoked. Again we can illustrate the meaning of this facet from the same example. If incentives are necessary then any attempt to establish equality of reward will be doomed to failure. Thus even if financial returns were equalised there would inevitably develop a system of informal inequalities from privileged access to goods in short supply to the size of the carpet on the floor of one's office. Human nature 'will out'. As the Latin poet Horace expressed it:

'Chase Nature away with a pitchfork, she'll hurry back
And in triumph burst unobserved through your morbid
refinement.'

(Epistles, I, x)

Social and political organisation has to accommodate itself to
human nature and not vice versa. The same holds for those who
deny the necessity of incentives. The conviction of these thinkers
that reorganisation of working practices (such as building cars in
teams and not on assembly lines) is feasible, rests on regarding such
practices as compatible with or (more strongly) as an expression of
human nature.

To summarise, my claim is that if the concept of human nature is
examined it can be seen to possess these three facets. As the use of a
single example aimed to demonstrate these, as facets, are
interrelated. Accordingly, what is deemed suitable or appropriate
human action is conditioned by what is held to be given in human
nature and whether an attribute has this quality of givenness is part
and parcel of judging whether it occurs universally. Of course, that
the concept of human nature does have these facets is my
interpretation. The vindication of this interpretation will have to lie
in the treatment I provide in the following chapters.

These chapters take the following form. Chapter 1 provides
concrete illustrative material, gleaned from historical and
contemporary political theory, of the way 'human nature' functions
in political debate. The deliberately schematic treatment will show
not only some of the ways in which political issues and an
understanding of human nature interact but will also thereby
provide miniature case-studies to complement the succeeding
chapters. The heart of the book consists of an examination of the
three facets. To make the argument easier to digest the treatment of
each facet is spread over two or three linked chapters. Hence
Chapters 2 and 3 deal with practicality; Chapters 4, 5, and 6 with
universality and Chapters 7 and 8 with givenness. Though broken up
in this way it is important to remember that because these are three
facets then the discussion in these chapters should not be
understood independently or discretely. Throughout this discussion
I am not committing myself to the tenability of the concept. In
Chapter 9 I look briefly at two arguments that question its
tenability. I conclude, however, by providing some observations as

to why a notion of human nature seems indispensable but end on the cautionary note that the notion cannot function as an ultimate 'problem-solver'. In as much as it has a message, this book argues that the self-evidence implied by the term's general usage is deceptive; it does not offer an easy way out of difficulties. There is no short cut to hard thinking and that includes thinking about human nature. Finally I should clarify my terminology and stylistic conventions. I use the terms 'Man' and 'human nature' interchangeably. The former is capitalised to indicate that it refers to both male and female. In general I have tried to avoid personal pronouns. When citing others I have followed their conventions.

It is always difficult to identify retrospectively where a particular idea came from. I used 'human nature' without subjecting the term to any extensive analysis as a *leitmotif* for my study of Hume and Hegel (Berry, 1982) – a work very different from this. I first began to think seriously about the concept itself in the context of an extra-mural class on Human Nature which I gave for two years in the late 1970s. In 1980 I gave a semester course entitled 'Human Nature' at the College of William and Mary in Williamsburg, Virginia. During this period I began to contemplate a book. My original plans have changed dramatically, but for its publication in its current form I am grateful to Peter Jones and Albert Weale, the editors of this series, who provided me with a platform by agreeing to my suggestion that it would find a suitable home in their project. More importantly I am grateful to them both for their detailed comments and suggestions upon my manuscript, from which I have profited greatly. I am grateful also to Michael Lessnoff for reading a draft of Chapter 1, to Manchester's Political Theory Seminar for listening to and commenting upon a version of Chapter 2 and to my colleagues in a workshop on Human Nature that I directed under the auspices of the European Consortium for Political Research in Salzburg 1984 for their views on a version of Chapter 7. The preparation of my text through its various stages has been the responsibility of Elspeth Shaw, Avril Johnstone and Barbara Fisher – to each of whom I am happy to record publicly my thanks.

The final word must be familial. Craig and Paul by ensuring that matters were kept in proportion helped make this book possible and Christine helped to make it seem worthwhile.

Christopher J. Berry

1 Human Nature and Political Argument

My aim in this chapter is to survey a number of the ways in which the questions of human nature and politics intersect. By indicating the range of this intersection the claim that human nature is a significant topic in the comprehension and explanation of politics will gain some plausibility. While the following chapters will concern themselves with a more or less formal analysis of the concept of human nature itself and why it should have bearing upon politics, this chapter itemises some of the ways in which human nature does bear on politics.

A necessary condition for an issue to be political is that it is the subject of dispute or debate. Given that this is the case, I shall use the notion of dispute as a way of structuring this survey. Politics and human nature will be treated as intersecting in four areas of dispute and argument. The extent and ways in which Man is (1) an individual or communitarian being, (2) a political or apolitical being, (3) a free rational or determined arational being, (4) a perfectible or imperfectible being.

I have chosen these four polarities for two reasons. Firstly, they each can be seen to be 'live' issues in contemporary political argument and, secondly, they each have a long 'history' behind them. In no way does this entail that these four polarities exhaust the ways in which divergent views of human nature can be classified. Also, it cannot be emphasised too strongly that these four polarities are *not* mutually exclusive. They cross-cut each other. This does mean that there is a certain artificiality in the presentation. There is, for example, a close connexion between James Mill's apolitical view of human nature and Hobbes's arational one although these are here treated discretely. It follows from this that no claim is being made for either thoroughness or completeness. The aim is to

1

provide some illustrative substantive material to complement the more formal analyses in the following chapters.

For each polarity the following strategy will be followed. I expound the key argument from each side via a brief discussion of one or two representative thinkers. I then take an example of a substantive dispute between the two arguments to illustrate how the differing views of human nature contribute to the nature and character of the dispute. Finally it must be stressed that it is the 'contribution' of human nature to political argument that is being surveyed and no claim is being made to the effect that disputes over 'human nature' are the sole source of political argument.

Individual/communitarian

Individual

The basic conception is that Man is an independent individual for whom group membership is voluntary.

The key argument for independence can be illustrated through the writings of John Locke. In Chapter 8 of his Second *Treatise of Government* (1965) Locke summarises his argument thus far as 'Man being, as has been said, by Nature, all free, equal and independent, no one can be put out of this Estate, and subjected to the Political Power of another, without his own Consent' (§95). By 'freedom' Locke means the ability of individuals to order their actions and dispose of their possessions as they themselves think fit without needing to ask the permission of any other individuals (§4). By 'equality' Locke means no individual has any more power or authority over another than they have over him or her. This equality is thus that of the natural freedom that each enjoys (§54). 'Independence' is a corollary of these two. No individual is morally or politically dependent on another. If this were not the case then there would be neither 'natural freedom' nor 'natural equality'. Locke's particular target was the patriarchalism of Robert Filmer (1949). Patriarchal doctrine taught that just as the physical dependence of the child upon its father was natural so too its political and moral dependence was natural. Hence, in explicit contrast to Locke, according to Filmer individuals (with the exception of kings who are the 'fathers of their people') are born subjects.

Locke does not deny that humans are born physically dependent nor does he deny the importance of the family as a socialising institution but he does not wish to make those facts salient or significant (the importance of a fact of human nature being 'salient' will be explored in Chapter 2). Instead, he focuses on the freedom and equality of individuals which stems from their possession of reason (§63). It is by use of their reason that individuals are able to act as independent agents. Reason, however, takes time to mature and during the period of its immaturity (childhood) the individual is under the care and protection of its family (§65). But once the 'age of reason' has been attained, every individual is a free, equal and independent agent able to make their own decisions. For some other person to take a decision on the part of another who is rational is to abrogate the latter's freedom and equality. The significance of this can be seen in the two spheres that most concerned Locke – the political and the religious.

Political power is defined by Locke as the right of making laws (with penalties of death) for the public good (§3). We have to ask how this power can be exercised among individuals who are free, equal and independent. The only way this exercise is possible is for those who are subject to the law to consent to be subject (§22) and since all are equal then all must be subject (§142). Given that individuals are naturally free, equal and rational, then no individual would consent to a situation that was injurious to that freedom (for no rational individual would change their current situation for a worse one (§131)). This has two significant implications. Firstly, obedience to a law to which consent has been given is not an infringement of liberty but a preservation and enlargement of it (§57). Secondly, an exercise of political power that was injurious to equality and liberty would not gain the consent of individual subjects. Such exercise would thus be illegitimate. Whoever exercises illegitimate power may be legitimately removed and replaced by a body who will be trusted to preserve property (§222), by which Locke means the right to life, liberty and estates (§123).

Though it is important to Locke's argument that membership of civil society (where political power is exercised) is voluntary it is clear that the problem concerns the legitimacy of that power rather than whether or not individuals can subsist outside such a civil order. The task of this order is to preserve the life, liberty and property of its citizens. It is, however, no part of the duties of this order to take care of individuals' souls. This brings us to the religious sphere. This sphere is an integral part of the individual's independence. No one can compel another as to their religious convictions. Individuals seek the pursuit of their religious interests by means of a church. The crucial definition of a church that Locke supplies is 'a voluntary society of men joining themselves together of their own accord in order to the public worshipping of God in such a manner as they judge acceptable to him' (1948, p.129). As a voluntary association a church (its members) can decide how it is going to conduct its business but, equally, it can have no jurisdiction over those who have chosen not to belong to it. The latter must be tolerated.

Individuals choose to join a church (and by extension other groups) to further their own ends, which, as free independent beings, they are presumed to know better than anyone else. Members of a group thus share the pursuit of the same ends but these ends are specifiable independently of group membership. I don't become interested in tennis by being a member of a tennis club, it is because I am interested that I join the club. We can say therefore that such membership is an instrumental means to the realisation of an individually defined goal. Man is an individual.

Communitarian

The basic conception here is that human beings are constituted by the social relationships in which they are necessarily to be found.

The key argument for Man as a communitarian being can be illustrated through the writings of Karl Marx. For Marx, Man truly understood is a creative producer. But this is not an individual attribute because 'the essence of man is the true community of man, men by activating their own essence, produce, create this human community, this social being which is no abstract, universal power standing over against the solitary individual but is the essence of every individual, his own activity, his own life, his own spirit, his own wealth' (1975, p.265). When this essence is realised then individuals will be truly bonded; they will *not* relate to each other in terms of individually chosen ends in pursuit of separate interests. To produce as an authentic human being is to express this deep communality. Not only would such production be an expression of an individual's own activity but this individual would have in this productive activity satisfied the needs of another human being. Further, by satisfying the needs of another, this other acknowledges the producer as a complement, indeed as an 'essential part' of their own self. Through attaining this complementarity with another this individual has realised their 'human communal nature'. This whole process would of course be mutual so that 'our productions would be as many mirrors from which our natures would shine forth' (1975, pp.277–8).

This communal production expresses the distinctiveness of humans. It exhibits what Marx calls man's 'species-being' (1975, p.327ff). Animals, like ants and beavers, may well produce but they lack the self-consciousness and universality that humans possess. While ants produce under the compulsion of physical need, humans produce freely – indeed they also produce 'in accordance with the laws of beauty'. An object of beauty is not 'something' which is enjoyed only by the individual but is that which evokes a response from all humans. Through communal production humans can therefore contemplate themselves as communal beings in the products of that production.

If Man is truly a deeply communal being then it is a mistake to conceive of community as optional. The only way that is possible is by conceiving of an individual in isolation – as an atom or a self-sufficient monad. From the perspective of such isolation community will appear as a threat because other individuals are perceived as limitations on freedom and not as agents of the realisation of that freedom. But such a perspective is a distortion because it is only achieved by suppressing human sociality and regarding Man as somehow possessing interests and rights without yet being a social creature. Though these sentiments are expressed most openly in Marx's early writings they do recur throughout his work. The crucial point we can also find being made in the *Grundrisse* for example, 'The human being is an animal which can individuate itself only in the midst of society. Production by an isolated individual outside society . . . is . . . an absurdity' (1973, p.84).

Community is thus not some optional extra (like some large tennis club), but is definitive or constitutive in that outside this arena the individual is an unreal abstraction. It is a distortion therefore to premise any statement about the real concrete nature of social life on statements about individuals. Since this is a proposition about human nature it means that it holds good universally for all humans (see Chapter 4). Accordingly all humans need other humans to achieve their humanity. Their interrelation is thus one of basic complementarity. To realise one's ends genuinely is to appreciate that these ends incorporate the ends of others not as mere means but as a necessary element in being able to formulate 'ends' in the first place. I couldn't have an interest in tennis unless there were other (pre-existing) tennis players. Left to one's own devices, bereft of community, the individual would lack any sense of self. Without others we would not know who 'we are'. Man is a communitarian being.

Argument

Out of the many areas of dispute where this distinction between conceiving Man as an individual and Man as a communitarian being can be seen to feature, I have chosen the question of distributive justice. The crucial question in this debate is: what principles should govern the distribution of 'goods' (including rights, liberties as well as material possessions) in a society? In short, what is a just society?

The individualist answer, as illustrated by Robert Nozick (1974), is that the only legitimate principles are those that result from the processes of individuals acting and choosing freely. This position, in its turn, rests on the principle that 'individuals are inviolable' (p.31). The practical significance of this is that 'no moral balancing act can take place among us; there is no moral overweighing of one of our lives so as to lead to a greater overall *social* good' (p.33: Nozick's emphasis). Individuals are 'separate existences' and, as 'distinct individuals', they are 'not resources for us'. Nozick believes that any attempt to distribute the goods of society according to some predetermined pattern (such as moral merit, needs, intelligence) will infringe the rights of some individuals. He thinks this because on his interpretation to operate such a pattern will require continuous interference in people's lives in order to prevent them performing actions that will upset the pattern (p.163). I, as a free individual, should be able to do as I wish with my justly acquired property and not have that freedom curtailed by others in the name of some social good. For Nozick there can be no central distributive agency in a free society because such an agency would assume that the resources of separate individuals in that society were part of some common pool to be distributed according to some favoured principle. In a free society, by contrast, what each person gets is obtained from others through exchange or gift (p.149). In short, in a just society, setting aside the acquisition of any goods previously unheld, distribution will be 'from each as they choose, to each as they are chosen' (p.160).

It is clear, as Nozick openly acknowledges, that his theory hinges on an essentially Lockean understanding of human nature. Individuals are exactly that; they are discrete entities. This discreteness constitutes a moral claim because it is as individuals that humans possess inviolable rights.

It is not difficult to see how working from a communitarian view of human nature the question of the proper distribution of social goods will be answered differently. In an important sense the very question of distribution mis-states the situation in that it assumes in its formulation the individualistic perspective. Brian Barry acknowledges this when he invokes the notion of 'altruistic collaboration' as a principle of right human relationships to which questions of the right distribution are morally subordinate (1973, pp.167–8). In similar fashion Alison Jaggar remarks that 'the concern with justice remains a typically liberal preoccupation, in so far as it rests on a conception of society as composed of essentially separate individuals, each competing with the others for their "fair share" ' (1983, p.175).

Nevertheless we can sketch out a model of social justice that operates from communitarian premises. If the individual is 'not a given but is a social construction' (Parekh, 1982, p.190) then this 'social' component is a constitutive ingredient. Without society individuals would not be what they are. Though he himself still operates within an essentially individualist framework, John Rawls gives expression to the key point here with his notion of 'collective assets'. Individuals possess differing natural talents and since these are 'natural' then they are declared by Rawls to be undeserved and thus provide no justifiable ground for social advantage (1972, pp.101–2). Rather these talents are to be regarded as a collective asset the benefits of which should accrue not to the contingent individuals who happen to possess or enjoy them but to the community as a whole (cf. p.179).

The crucial point here can be pursued further. What is regarded as a 'talent' depends on the particular nature of the community in question. Thus, in a society which values technology, any individual with a 'natural bent' towards mechanical inventiveness will be valued whereas in a different sort of society, say that of a self-denying religious order, such a bent would not be valued and another 'trait' such as, say, a quality of holiness would be valued. Furthermore any individual gift or ability still requires the co-operation of others in order for it to be effectively exercised. Capablanca was a prodigy but for him to fulfil himself depended on others recognising this and this recognition itself is inseparable from the prior existence of the game of chess with its elaborate rules and of institutions like World Championships, which enabled this genius to be put to 'use'. If this holds good for something as extra-ordinary as natural genius then it holds *a fortiori* for each and every individual in a society.

It follows from these communitarian premises about human nature that a just society is – according to Michael Meacher (1977, p.136) – one where the members of that society govern their interrelationships by the ideals of 'sharing, cooperation, altruism'. The values of a just society are accordingly characterised by Meacher as 'more equal sharing of the material benefits of society, greater sharing in the key decisions rather than subjection to artificial hierarchies of command, and greater sharing of opportunities to develop one's full potentials'. This society, he continues, also 'abhors class domination and individualist self-aggrandizement at the expense of others'. In short, only in a society manifesting these values can 'the fullness of man's true nature' be realised.

In essence, therefore, the argument over the definition of a just society, and implicit within it the great debate between the merits of capitalism and socialism, can be seen to have as one of its ingredients divergent views of the nature of Man. Nor, arguably, is this a minor ingredient. Rather, if it is accepted that Man is pre-eminently an individual and that this has moral (individuals have rights), epistemological (individuals alone know who they are and what they want) and ontological (all human collectivities are reducible to their components – the individual) significance, then taxation of earnings, as an instrument to redistribute income, may well be characterised, as Nozick does, as forced labour (1974, p.164). Deny that significance and this characterisation loses any persuasive appeal. Conversely, if it is accepted that Man is pre-eminently a communitarian being, and that this has moral (the common good is my good), epistemological (knowledge is a social product) and ontological ('no man is an island') significance, then it can be proposed, as Meacher does, that the State can have powers of job placement (1977, p.140). Once again, deny the significance and this proposal appears as an inexcusable infringement of an individual's right to determine his or her occupation. The upshot is that in the political debate over 'what is a just society?', conflicting views of the nature of Man play a key role. In particular, whichever concept of human nature is held will be crucial in making one side in the debate appear more plausible than the other.

Political/apolitical

Political

The basic conception here is that Man is an active political agent whose humanity is realised through such activity.

The key argument here can be illustrated in its principles by Aristotle's account of citizenship. Aristotle sees Man as 'by nature an animal intended to live in the polis' (1946, p.5). This is a technical definition. By 'nature' Aristotle means the end, goal or purpose (*telos*) of a 'thing' – so the nature of a knife is that it cuts not that it is made of metal: a good knife is one that performs its defining function well. By 'polis' is meant the political community within which the individual dwells. Life outside the polis is an isolated life which is the prerogative of either beasts or gods and not humans. Humans (this is to generalise Aristotle's own account) only therefore exhibit their humanity when acting politically, which means in association with other humans. To say that political activity is natural is also (it follows from Aristotle's definitions) to say that it is an activity that constitutes an end or fulfils a purpose. This natural political activity is thus self-sufficient activity; it is done for its own sake. We do not fulfil our nature as political beings when political action is viewed as a *means* of attaining something else – just as a knife no longer fulfils its purpose as a knife when it is put on a wall to serve as a decoration.

There are for our purposes two significant consequences of this essentially Aristotelian position. The first of these is that it permits a ranking of activities between those which are self-sufficient and those which are instrumental. One of Aristotle's own examples of this ranking is his downgrading of commercial activity. According to Aristotle, merchants should not ideally be allowed to enjoy the privileges of citizenship. His reasoning behind this is that those who *depend* on others for their livelihood (as a shopkeeper depends on his customers) are engaged in that task not incidentally but centrally. The consequence of this centrality is that their habits, dispositions and frames of mind (their 'virtues') are constrained by the demands of their occupation. They have no time to indulge in pursuits like politics which are worthy of pursuit for their own sake. The grocer sells cabbages to obtain money to buy the other things he *must* have in order to live. Accordingly he is unable to participate in the 'good life' – a life of freedom and *independence* from the demands of necessity. The grocer's life, because it is in this way 'inimical to goodness' (1946, p.301), does not manifest a fully realised or truly human life. This human life constitutes the good life which is the life of political activity. Thus in 'doing politics' – in debating, judging and generally taking decisions that effect every citizen's well-being – Man is exercising the definitive character that constitutes human nature.

The second consequence is that if politics is intrinsically worthwhile, because it realises Man's natural capacity as a political being, then there is no way that this activity can be delegated. No-one else can 'do politics' for you by proxy. To be a citizen for Aristotle meant enjoying the rights of sharing in deliberative or judicial office (p.95). This means, and this is what is crucial for our particular purposes, that there is a conceptual connexion between activities that realise human nature and political participatory activity. In doing the latter the former is achieved. Conversely failure to partake in the latter means that the former has not been attained. Though as we have seen there are gradations, the extremes are represented by the citizen on the one hand and the slave on the other. Slaves are slaves as a fact of nature in so far as they are incapable of independent existence, and thus incapable of living a political life (1946, p.11). Man, however, is naturally not a slave: Man is a political being.

Apolitical

The basic conception here is that human beings are instrumental functional creatures who act so as best to satisfy their own interests. The key argument for Man as an apolitical being can be gleaned from James Mill's *Essay on Government* (1955). Mill's whole enterprise rests on the conviction that the 'acts of men will be conformable to their interests' (p.84) and these interests can be discerned by a 'scientific' account of human nature. The crux of this account is that 'every human being is determined by his pains and pleasures and that his happiness corresponds with the degree in which his pleasures are great and his pains are small' (p.48). To achieve such happiness Man desires wealth and power and, since happiness is always desired, then the desire for wealth and power is limitless (p.63). Due to this 'every man who has not all the objects of his desire has inducement to take them from any other man who is weaker than himself'. Accordingly there is a need for government whereby a 'great number of men combine and delegate to a small number the power necessary for protecting them all' (pp.49–50). But any individual who is in power will, because human nature is universal, also seek wealth and power. There is a need for checks and balances. The most effective device to that end is a system of representation. The community choose representatives to govern them. Significantly, the key question regarding government has now become how to restrain it. Mill never considers government as anything other than a *means* and is thus interested solely in its instrumental efficiency: it must be strong enough to check its subjects and yet itself must be constrained against using its power mischievously (p.67). What government does (when suitably constrained) is to assist humans in attaining the objects of their desire.

These objects (given the human lot) depend on the necessity of labour. Labour itself rests on property. This is because ownership of property supplies the owners with the security that they will be able to enjoy the fruits of their labour; the benefits will accrue to them and not another (p.54). Any concern with politics is thus derivative in a two-fold sense. Firstly, government is looked upon as the means to maintain some security of possession and, secondly, any involvement in government affairs is prompted by the desire to keep this 'means' operating efficiently.

We can gain further insight into why this picture of Man portrays humans as apolitical by noting, firstly, why Mill invested 'power' with such importance and, secondly, how he proposed that representation should be achieved. All humans desire power because the powerful are able to make others with less power do as they are told. If it is held to be axiomatic that humans seek to avoid pain then it follows that each will desire that others do the painful activities. The master/slave relationship is thus the seeming quintessence of human relationships with the masters using their power to make the slaves undertake the painful tasks. The slaves for their part will strive to obtain power to force others to do these tasks. This is in direct contrast to Aristotle because according to him natural slaves recognised that their *telos* was realised in obedience (so that there could indeed be an element of friendship between master and slave (1946, p.17)). Conversely for Mill since the interests of masters and slaves were fundamentally opposed it means that the master must always use his power to oppress the resentful slave so that their relationship is one of incessant cruelty (1955, p.60). Politics which for Aristotle was a relationship between equals and the expression of their shared participation in the good life for the sake of all, is for Mill an extension of power where, unless checked, the rulers will plunder the ruled. This Mill affirms is a 'grand governing law of human nature' (p.56).

As we saw Mill regards the institution of representation as the best means of controlling governmental abuse. The guiding task is to ensure identity of interest between the representers and the represented. Given that it is *interest* that is decisive then Mill is immediately able to state that women may be disqualified because their interests are taken care of by either their husbands or their fathers. Furthermore all males under forty can be deemed to have their interests taken care of by older males. This last point is defended by Mill invoking another 'law of human nature'; this time to the effect that fathers regard their sons' interests as an essential part of their own (p.75). What is important from our perspective is not Mill's consistency but Mill's governing thought that the interests of the excluded are still being heeded. If this is so then there is nothing to be gained by them, or for them, if they were actually included in political activity. Exclusion is no great pain: Man is apolitical.

Argument

I have chosen the debate over the meaning of democracy to illustrate the dispute between political and apolitical views of human nature. The crucial question in this debate is: what are the appropriate criteria to apply when judging whether or not a polity or institution is truly democratic?

If Man is judged to be a political animal then in contemporary debate this has meant that the test of democracy is the degree of citizen participation. Carole Pateman outlines the theory of participatory democracy as follows. Democracy cannot be confined to the periodic election of representatives at the national level but must foster the development in the citizens of the requisite individual attitudes and psychological qualities. This fostering will come from the act of participating not only in local government but also in spheres like industry which impinge directly on daily life. Such participation is educative. This makes a participatory system self-sustaining because the qualities necessary to support it are generated by the very act of participation itself (1970, pp.42–3).

The reasons why participation has this potential and how it relies on an understanding of human nature are developed by Peter Bachrach. To Bachrach a participatory democracy enables individuals to gain in self-esteem and permits a growth toward a fuller affirmation of their personalities (1969, p.101). Participatory democracy has these effects because it recognises the self-developmental character of the individual. But further, and more significantly, Bachrach holds that this self-development will reveal to individuals their true identity and what it is they really want (1975, p.41). Like Pateman, Bachrach wishes to extend the political arena beyond national elections. Of course, Pateman and Bachrach see democracy as a means of exercising control but to them it is less a means to an end than an intrinsically worthwhile form of activity whereby individuals can realise themselves. This means, to give Bachrach's own examples, that political activity is not on a par with sailing, money-making or theatre-going but is an activity that enables the individual to develop into a 'socially conscious human being' and by developing in this way individuals express their true political human nature (1975, p.52).

However, if it is assumed that politics is not so central to human nature then a very different evaluation of democracy can follow.

Joseph Schumpeter, for example, holds that what makes democracy distinctive is its institutional arrangements whereby the individuals who are to make political decisions are chosen by a competitive struggle for people's votes (1950, p.269). Democracy is seen simply as a method of arriving at a government. The role of citizens (electors) is confined to choosing between rival sets of leaders. Schumpeter is quite explicit that this process is what 'democracy' *means* (p.285). He holds further that between elections the voters should exercise 'self-control', that is, they ought to acknowledge that political action is the business of those elected and not theirs (p.295). The exercise of this self-control will not be difficult because most people are apolitical. In a section of his book entitled 'Human Nature in Politics' Schumpeter observes that individuals are only rational and informed about what interests them and that politics does not fall into that category.

   This general relegation of the importance of political life is also maintained by Robert Dahl. Dahl invokes 'nature' to explain why, though they are found in social groups, humans are not in the main political; it is a fact that 'man is not by instinct a reasonable, reasoning, civic-minded being' (1970a, p.80). Hence many find political activity less gratifying than activity that relates to 'family, friends, recreation and the like' (p.79). The significant implication is that such individuals are not to be thought of as in some way failing to realise their humanity if they seek gratification in non-political activity. This apolitical view of human nature proposed by Dahl conditions his view of democracy. People will only become involved in politics if they feel intensely about an issue and the democratic political process (between periodic elections) takes the form of bargaining between groups of individuals who do feel intensely about some issue. If people do not exhibit political activity in their behaviour then it can be assumed that they are content to devote themselves to non-political activities (1956, p.134).

   We can take this final point to summarise the link between a view of human nature and a view of democracy. Bachrach criticises Dahl (1970b), because he conceives participation merely in instrumental terms. It is (for Dahl) a 'cost' in the economic sense that time is a scarce commodity so that to participate means forgoing other activities. It is thus (on Bachrach's gloss) a question of calculation – will it 'pay' to participate? But to Bachrach participation is not a cost but an activity of self-understanding; an activity whereby the participants will understand themselves as political beings. This is why Bachrach is able to hold that it is doubtful if the actual political preferences articulated by citizens in a less than fully participatory democracy are a true expression of their real interests (1975, p.47). Apathy, lack of involvement, rather than indicating the contentment of an essentially apolitical nature as Dahl would have it, is indicative of a frustration of the basic political character of human nature. Hence, when analysed these assessments of political apathy will reveal the crucial presence of conflicting views of the inter-relationship of human nature and political activity.

Free rational/determined arational

Free rational

The basic conception here is that human beings are uniquely rational beings in virtue of which they are self-conscious and free.

The view that Man is rational has been perhaps the most commonly held interpretation of human nature in Western culture, though it is not confined to the West; for example, that humans uniquely possess as their most important faculty an evaluating mind is also crucial in Confucian thought. The particular variant I have chosen to represent this understanding of human nature is that put forward by Hegel. According to Hegel the 'fundamental character of human nature' is Man's ability to think (1975, p.50). This ability sets up an unbridgeable gulf between humanity and animality: brutes lack that which Man necessarily possesses, thought. It is because, in essence, Man knows himself to be an animal that he ceases for that reason to be an animal (Hegel gives as an example Man's ability to turn the animal function of digestion, which humans possess along with pigs, into a science (1970, p.115)).

To say that Man alone can think is also to say that Man uniquely is free. I as a free agent can determine my own actions because I can think of myself as doing something other than that upon which I am currently engaged. This is illustrated by the human possibility of suicide (1942, p.43). No animal can commit suicide or even maim itself because its behaviour is not free but is determined by instincts, chief among which is its instinct for self-preservation. Humans as free rational agents are able not only to overcome externally determined constraints but can also impose constraints on themselves. These self-imposed constraints rather than being inimical to freedom are a manifestation of it. In marriage, for example, the partners agree to self-restrict their freedom. This self-restriction is the imposition of the duty of fidelity on themselves and as such it is a true liberation (1942, p.111). This is because, in duty, they have liberated themselves from the demands of mere impulse (indiscriminate, animal, lust) and they have affirmed themselves as free agents. In Hegel's terminology they have attained substantive freedom (1942, p.107).

The attainment of this substantive freedom is the lynch-pin of Hegel's political philosophy. Law can *appear* as a restriction on liberty because it prevents individuals doing as they might wish. However, correctly understood, law is a human creation and as such it embodies human reason or free will. The whole panoply of institutions that characterise human life – property,· contract, punishment, morality, marriage, markets, courts, Parliaments and so on – are embodiments of freedom and reason. Whereas physical laws of nature, like the force of gravity, have to be accepted as valid simply as they are, human laws are subject to the assessment of thought since their validity stems not from their mere existence. What does determine that validity is the extent to which they realise freedom or the extent to which they are rational. All laws do this in some degree but human history is the history of the increasing rationality and universality of law – from one (the despot) being free to all being free in the modern state. Hence history for Hegel is the story of freedom (1942, p.216) and since Man is free then history is also the story of Man. In contrast to this progressiveness animals have no history. Bereft as they are of thought and freedom brutes are confined to the repetitiveness of Nature – one generation of pigs is like all other generations of pigs. Man transcends Nature; Man is rational.

Determined arational

The basic conception here is that Man is an affective or passionate being whose major motivations escape control.

This concept of human nature can be illustrated by Hobbes's arguments in *Leviathan* (1914), the opening book of which is entitled 'Of Man'. Life is conceived by Hobbes to be but 'motions of limbs' (p.1). Two sorts of motion are identified: vital motion, such as the circulation of the blood, and voluntary or animal motion, such as running, which is preceded by an internal motion called 'endeavour'. There are two categories of endeavour – movement toward the something that causes it (appetite) and movement away (aversion). Since to be alive is always to be in motion, there will be constant movement – what Hobbes calls 'deliberation' – among these appetites and aversions. When an ostensible movement like running occurs it means that these internal movements have arrived at a decision. This decision is the act of willing. Hobbes thus defines will as 'the last appetite in deliberating' (p.29). These deliberations are all governed by the need to remain in motion and, as such, are all directed to an animal's own benefit. This is a fact of nature (p.99). Accordingly when an animal runs, it is acting on will, which is product of some determining appetite or aversion, to achieve some 'good' for itself. Hobbes is clear that this process refers to all animals and not exclusively to Man.

Hobbes does allow that only humans can speak (p.17). Words or names serve to register the consequences of our thoughts. Hobbes retains in his own distinctive way the classical connexion between language and reason when he defines reason as the reckoning of the consequences of agreed upon general names (p.18). However, what is crucial is the role Hobbes allots to reason. Reason is purely a capacity for calculation, in no way does it constitute a motive for action. Where there is no scope for adding or subtracting there is nothing for reason to do (p.19). Indeed for most individuals their reason is of little use to them in their 'common life' (p.21). The significant point is that Hobbes makes reason subordinate to demands of the appetites and aversions to ensure self-preservation. Whatever action is most conducive to our benefit is that which is to be judged the most reasonable. A consequence of this is that no human can be said to act reasonably if by so doing they jeopardise their own existence (p.75). Suicide it now follows is an act of madness (1840, p.88).

What determines human behaviour therefore are appetites and aversions, fears, hopes, desires or, in general, passions. It is these passions that produce a natural condition of war of all against all and it is these passions that motivate Man to seek remedy. Reason can provide some general rules whereby peace can be established, but these are helpless against Man's natural passions so that the only way peace will be attained and maintained is by use of the strongest passion of all, namely, fear of violent death to be wielded by an absolute sovereign who will terrorise (1914, p.89) all subjects into peaceful behaviour.

To say that human behaviour is determined is to say it is necessitated. A human must act to preserve him or herself – the condemned will resist their executioner whereas the martyr is in the grip of another delusory passion. Hobbes, however, still maintains that humans are free. Freedom or liberty 'in the proper sense' is freedom from external physical constraints (1914, p.111). Wherever humans are not constrained there they are free. This means that all law is an inhibition upon free activity. Man's behaviour is thus 'free' in so much as it emanates from his or her own will but whatever was willed was determined by a precedent cause (passion) and that cause was determined by one precedent to that and so on in a continuous chain of cause and effect. Man is thus an arational creature of passion whose behaviour is determined.

Argument

I have chosen the debate over the justification of punishment to illustrate the divergent prescriptions that stem from conceiving of human nature as either free and rational or as determined and arational. Punishment appears to require justification because it necessarily involves the deliberate infliction of pain (or at least the restriction of choice as in the paying of a fine) and, without further reason, this infliction is morally objectionable. There are a number of justifications that can be offered and the difference between them can easily be related to differences in conceptions of human nature.

If humans are held to be rational self-conscious beings, then this means that they are responsible for their actions. As rational I am capable of knowing that a state of affairs exists (a law) and I am capable of knowing the consequences of my actions should I concern myself with that state (be eligible for justified infliction of pain). Should I decide to take no action then I also know that inaction too will have consequences (no punishment). If, being aware of these factors, I then proceed of my own free volition to take my neighbour's apples without her permission, I can be said to *deserve* my punishment. Punishment on these grounds is therefore justified because of the guilt of an offender and an offender is deemed guilty if he or she acted knowingly in breaking a legitimate law. Though this is a simplified account we have here the germ of the retributivist justification of punishment. While their terminology is different, many contemporary defenders of the retributivist justification are reiterating Hegel's argument (1942, p.69ff).

It follows from this retributivist account that if an individual acted unknowingly then there is no guilt and if there is no guilt there can be no justification for punishment. It is in this way that the distinction is drawn between the kleptomaniac who steals under some compulsion and the pickpocket who conscientiously chooses to steal. This example serves to introduce the nub issue. Hegel and his contemporary followers would regard this distinction as meaningful and would, in general, regard the kleptomaniac as the exceptional case. Of course in practice disputes over the appropriateness of punishment are more intensely debated over apparently more contentious cases: are the circumstances of a 'broken home', living in a 'run-down' neighbourhood, receiving insufficient schooling such as to diminish the responsibility, and hence the guilt, of a teenage 'vandal'? But since conceptual clarity is more likely to come from extremes it will be more fruitful to take B. F. Skinner as an example of a deterministic theory of human nature as arational and to contrast his views on punishment with that of the retributivists with their view of the rationality of human nature.

In his brief, essentially polemical, work *Beyond Freedom and Dignity* (1973) Skinner criticises the advocates of what he calls Autonomous Man. Retributivists are advocates of Autonomous Man. It is a view of Man as an initiator who, as the possessor of free-will, creates internally the behaviour that we observe externally. But to Skinner this is a reflection of ignorance and tantamount to a belief in miracles (p.19). Human behaviour just like any other phenomenon in nature has antecedent causes which necessarily determine certain effects. In place of this pre-scientific belief in autonomy Skinner holds that behaviour is shaped by its consequences. In his terminology behaviour is subject to a process of 'operant-conditioning'. Food by satisfying hunger positively reinforces the behaviour so that next time hunger is felt food will be

sought. There are also negative reinforcers (which Skinner, in
Hobbesian language, calls 'aversive'). For example, the reduction
in heat achieved by moving into the shade from the hot sun is
repeated since, in the past, that movement has had the effect of
reducing the unpleasantness of too much heat. Behaviour is
explained by reference to the environment and thus this 'scientific
analysis shifts both the responsibility and the achievement to the
environment' (p.30).

This conclusion has bearing on punishment. The questions which
the retributivist supposes to be central, such as intention or
premeditation, can be restated in terms of the environment to which
a person has been exposed. Accordingly, properly understood
'what a person "intends to do" depends upon what he has done in
the past and what has then happened' (p.75). All human behaviour
is controlled, or operantly conditioned, so that what the
retributivist labels as a free, rational act of self-determination is not
a free act at all because such an act is controlled; there were causes
at work determining why that particular action rather than another
was undertaken. Legal punishment is simply one form of control
and, indeed, it has proved to be ineffective. A better solution to
crime is to adopt an appropriate technology of behaviour (p.148). If
it is the environment which is the crucial then it is that which should
be changed. Since all human behaviour is controlled in some way it
is not sensible to rejoin to this proposal that it infringes human
freedom or dignity, for such freedom or dignity does not exist in the
way that the rationalist portrays it. There is accordingly no
justification for punishment for there is, in the requisite sense, no
responsible agent. Man like any other animal is quite explicitly for
Skinner a machine; an extraordinarily complex machine, it is
granted, but a machine nonetheless (p.197).

This view is patently at odds with that put forward by Hegel. Such
is the gulf between them that, as is exemplified in the case of
punishment, they are scarcely disputing about the same issue at all.
Such a conclusion usefully makes a point that will concern us in later
chapters, namely, that when conceptions of human nature are at
odds it is difficult to discern any way of reconciling them, though
that is not to say that they are beyond criticism. A theory of human
nature serves to establish what factors will be deemed relevant to an
issue so that a different theory can produce quite different criteria of
relevance and hence address itself to quite different factors.

Perfectible/imperfectible

Perfectible

The basic conception here is that human beings are able to make the world after their own image and this is because Man possesses the capacity to surmount any supposed external obstacle.

This perfectibilist reading of human nature will be illustrated chiefly from the writing of William Godwin (1976). Godwin accepted Locke's argument that the human mind is originally a blank sheet and its corollary that all knowledge was the product of subsequent experience. Having accepted this Godwin pursued its implications rigorously. Human character is the product of education if this is understood in its widest sense to mean 'every incident that produces an idea in the mind' (p.111). Children it follows from this can be likened to a 'ductile and yielding substance' which can be 'moulded into conformity with our wishes' (p.112). Children, and all humans, are presumed by Godwin to possess the capacity to apprehend truth *and* to act upon it. Humans are so constituted, Godwin declares, that 'nothing is necessary but to show us that a thing is truly good and worthy to be desired in order to excite in us a passion for its attainment' (p.137). This means that truth is omnipotent; it will triumph over vice and moral weakness. The consequence of this omnipotence is that 'man is perfectible or in other words susceptible of perpetual improvement' (p.140). Furthermore this improvement contains within itself the source of its perpetuity. Since vice and weakness are the product of ignorance and error it means they are the product of an improper education. However once a proper education is instilled then its recipients will in their turn be able to instil truth into others and they into yet others and so on. The upshot is that the 'advocates of falsehood and mistake must continually diminish and well-informed adherents of truth incessantly multiply' (p.142).

What institutional consequences does Godwin see following from this perfectibility? Government is no more than a necessary evil and is only necessary because it is underpinned by ignorance and self-interest (p.168). Accordingly with the growth of truth throughout society so the principles of justice will grow and these will ultimately render government superfluous. Justice is 'no respecter of persons' and once this truth has been 'brought home' to the understanding then any preference with respect to ourselves or our kin will be seen not to be relevant (in a famous illustration Godwin holds that if it was in my power to save from death either my brother or Fenelon, I should choose the latter because of his greater contribution to mankind (p.170)). The most desirable state of mankind is that which makes the smallest encroachment on individual independence (p.76). This 'state' will be possible because the demands of justice will bring about equal admission of all to the means of improvement and pleasure (p.736).

There are no conceivable obstacles to this perfectibilism. It is true that humans are prone to habit but all habits originate in judgment and retain within them because of that an element which is susceptible to considerations of truth. As for native, or instinctive, endowments Godwin simply denies their existence. Any differences at birth are due to effects (experiences) received in the womb and to claim that self-preservation, for example, is innate is an error because we cannot prefer existence before we know from experience why it is preferable (p.103). Similarly self-love is nothing more than the awareness that some sensations are painful and others pleasant. The only obstacles are those that Man in ignorance has created. But with the growth of truth these obstacles will be removed so that in the vision of Godwin's French contemporary, Condorcet (1933, p.228f), there will be no inequality between individuals and no inequality between nations, all prejudices will be eradicated, peace will be the norm and though humans will remain mortal yet their lifespan will increase indefinitely. Man is perfectible.

Imperfectible

The basic conception here is that Man is a complex being. By 'complex' here I mean that human nature contains within it principles or aspects that are outside Man's control. There is an inner recalcitrance. Man is a complex being (rather than a simple or transparent being), who is inherently unable to attain complete self-mastery or guarantee that human action will turn out as intended.

There are various manifestations of this complexity. It is an important ingredient in the Christian doctrine of human sinfulness. This can be illustrated by the teaching of St. Augustine.

God is good and Man as God's creation enjoyed a life without need, without disease and violence and without desire or fear (1945, vol. 2, p.56). In return for this beneficence all God commanded was obedience. The disproportionality between the benefit and the cost was such that when Man disobeyed it was the height of injustice. What prompted this disobedience? Augustine's answer is pride. Man was too proud to owe obedience. Mankind thought themselves self-sufficient, thought of themselves as their own beginners and loved themselves and not God (vol. 2, p.43–4). The punishment for this presumption was that

'Man, who might have kept the command and been spiritual in body, became now carnal in mind; and because he had before delighted in his own pride, now he tasted God's justice; becoming not as he desired his own master, but falling even from himself, he became his slave that taught him sin, changing his sweet liberty into wretched bondage, being willingly dead in spirit, and unwilling to die in the flesh, forsaking eternal life, and condemned to death.' (vol. 2, p.45)

The nature of Man was changed irrevocably. Our human nature was now fixed. Man as now and permanently constituted is prey to desires and these desires represent an inner inescapable divisiveness with human nature. There is an unavoidable inner recalcitrance. Man now wants what cannot be had and has what is not wanted. Man is prey to lusts. Humans experience, for example, anger which is the lust for revenge, avarice which is the lust for money, boasting which is the lust for vain-glory and political ambition which is the lust for power (*libido dominandi*) (vol. 2, p.46). Man it is true does possess reason but although this distinguishes humans from beasts yet 'the mind itself wherein reason and understanding are natural inherents is weakened and darkened by the mists of inveterate error' (vol. 1, p.313). Man cannot therefore rely on reason and must have faith. Man is inherently flawed.

However, the imperfectibilist conception of human nature does not need to be couched in theological terms. This can be illustrated from the writings of Godwin's contemporaries, Edmund Burke and David Hume.

Burke (1882) states quite explicitly that 'the nature of Man is intricate' (p.334). What are the sources and manifestations of this intricacy? This question is easier to answer negatively: Man is intricate because humans are only imperfectly rational. Throughout the *Reflections* Burke attacks 'men of theory' who are variously described as sophisters, economists and calculators. Such men believe problems of government and policy are solvable just as the problems of arithmetic are solvable, namely, by the application of abstract reason. But such abstraction fails to heed the recalcitrance of human nature. Instead, a more accurate appraisal of human nature would reveal that instincts and natural sentiments play a large and socially significant role. Instincts and sentiments fortify the fallibility and frailty of reason (p.308) so that, by heeding what comes naturally, humans look upon kings with awe, parliaments with affection, magistrates dutifully, priests with reverence and nobles with respect (p.358). These sentiments are what Burke, quite deliberately, calls prejudices. Remove them, leaving nothing but abstract 'naked reason', and humans would be reliant on their own paltry stock of wisdom making them not only indecisive but anti-social. By contrast prejudice 'renders a man's virtue his habit and not a series of unconnected acts. Through just prejudice his duty becomes a part of his nature' (p.359). Chief amongst such prejudices is the Church for Man is 'by his constitution a religious animal' (p.363).

Any particular state of affairs can be judged from the viewpoint of an abstract truth as inadequate but it is the viewpoint that is in error. Reason, merely a part of Man, is being presumptuous in claiming with arithmetical certainty to legislate for the complex whole that constitutes human nature (p.452). The 'metaphysical and alchemistical legislators' reduce Man to 'loose counters merely for the sake of simple telling' and in so doing they ignore human nature. In particular, they ignore the diversifying effects of habits which establish 'second nature' (p.454). As Burke indicates with his use of this last phrase he does not regard habits as having an ancillary or superficial effect on human life but as having a deep and far-reaching impact.

Hume, to whom Burke is here clearly indebted, devoted much attention to the role played by habit. He declared in his *History of England* (1894) that 'habits more than reason we find in everything to be the governing principles of mankind' (vol. 3, p.116). To give one example of this principle in operation, though most governments originate in violence and usurpation (and would thus stand condemned at the bar of abstract reason) yet humans once they are *accustomed* to obedience do not think of departing from the path trodden by their ancestors (1963, p.87). Furthermore, since individuals are prone to habitual behaviour, the changes that have occurred in societies are better explained by gradual imperceptible alterations in customs and patterns of behaviour than they are by individual initiatives. Since customs are 'social facts' they go beyond individual control. The upshot of this is that no definable body of individuals intentionally or deliberately brought about the current situation. Hume, for example, attributes the growth in the power of the monarchy under Henry VII 'to habits of luxury' among the barons which caused them to dissipate their fortunes and thence their power (1894, vol. 2, p.602). The moral to be drawn is that there is no guarantee that contemporary plans and schemes will bring about their intended goal.

Human nature is of such a texture that the best laid plans 'gang aft agley'. We can predict that human nature will not conform predictably to fit a predesigned outcome. Since such a design is itself a human product it means that human nature is an 'obstacle' to itself. It is the very nature of this self-contradiction (which might be said to lie at the heart of Christian teaching of human sinfulness) that means that this obstacle can never be finally surmounted. Man is imperfectible.

Argument

I shall illustrate the divergence between perfectible and imperfectible views of human nature by examining an aspect of the debate between Isaiah Berlin and C. B. Macpherson on the nature of liberty.

Berlin distinguishes between two concepts of liberty. Negative liberty is the liberty from external inference or coercion; positive liberty is the liberty to be one's own master. Though these two concepts are admitted by Berlin to seem to be at 'no great logical distance from each other' yet their historical development has been marked by a sharp divergence (1969, pp.131–2). As a matter of 'historical fact' the doctrine of positive liberty has led to 'an authoritarian state obedient to the directions of an elite of Platonic guardians' (p.152). What Berlin sees underlying this reversal, whereby a doctrine of liberty has turned into a doctrine of authority, is the belief that all moral and political problems are solvable (p.145). This belief in its turn is held by Berlin to rest on the monistic assumption that the universe is governed by reason so that the rational solution to one problem cannot collide with the equally rational solution to another problem. Once this rational (final) solution has been found it will be recognised by all rational individuals. The upshot is an end to coercion and the domination of Man over Man (p.146).

This monism Berlin rejects. There is, he declares, no pattern whereby all values can be rendered harmonious (p.li, p.169). Rather, the ends of humans are many *and*, *pace* Condorcet whom Berlin cites here, they are not in principle all compatible. It is this rejection of harmony by Berlin that makes him in our terms an imperfectibilist. Berlin indeed echoes St. Augustine when he remarks that all monists 'assume that in a society of perfectly rational beings the lust for domination over men will be absent' (p.146).

Berlin's own imperfectibilist reading of human nature stems from his denial of ultimate compatibility. Instead Berlin holds firstly that humans must choose between absolute claims (p.169) (this is the human predicament (p.li)) and secondly that since it cannot be assumed that humans will make identical choices then it is a mistake to think that the possibility of conflict can ever be totally eliminated from human life. The consequence of this pluralism is that the negative concept of liberty, which insists on an inviolable minimum extent of individual liberty, is grounded 'deeply in the actual nature of men as they have developed through history' (p.165). Hence, given human nature (see Chapter 7) the negative concept is a 'truer and more humane ideal' (p.171). This moral superiority is enjoyed because the negative concept recognises that human goals are many. Not to recognise our diversity is to fail to acknowledge our imperfectibility. It is because we are imperfectible that we cannot attain some supposed perfect accord and cannot eliminate the potential for conflict and coercion. Since we are in this way permanently imperfect then the negative concept of liberty is to be preferred.

Macpherson by contrast wishes to defend an essentially positive concept of liberty. To him, negative liberty rests on an untenable view of human nature. This view Macpherson has labelled 'possessive individualism' and according to this doctrine the individual 'is seen as absolute proprietor of his own capacities, owing nothing to society for them. Man's essence is freedom to use his capacities in search of satisfactions' (1973, p.199), or more simply Man is viewed 'as essentially a consumer of utilities' (p.4). This consumption moreover is infinite; Man is always seeking satisfaction: desire is thus unlimited (p.17). Against this model of Man, Macpherson places a view of Man as an enjoyer or exerter of attributes and capacities; 'not a bundle of appetites seeking satisfaction but a bundle of conscious energies seeking to be exerted' (p.5). Liberty, it now follows for Macpherson, is better understood in terms of the liberty of Man to develop his powers and capacities (p.42).

Macpherson's perfectibilism stems from the assumptions he makes about the actual development of these powers. In essence he assumes, contrary to Berlin, that there is a basic homogeneity so that the development of individual human powers will not conflict. Macpherson openly admits that this is a 'staggering' assumption but nevertheless declares the assumption must be made (and he cites Condorcet as having made the same assumption (pp.54–5)). What consolidates Macpherson's perfectibilist credentials is that he provides an explanation of how on the one hand this assumption can appear staggering and on the other hand how it can be rationally expected to occur thus making it more than mere utopian speculation. It appears 'staggering' because scarcity has hitherto always been a given of the human condition and because 'possessive individualist' doctrines of infinite desire have mistakenly attributed this to an innate character of Man, when in fact it was only viewed approbatively because it served the needs of a capitalist market society (p.20). But Macpherson now believes the means are available to end true scarcity. Once this has been achieved (presumably by socialist governments organising production so that a spuriously controlled scarcity is no longer engineered by the need to make a profit) then a variety – Macpherson avers *pace* Berlin – of styles of life would emerge but which would not necessarily conflict (pp.111–12). The inevitability of conflict that Berlin, and other imperfectibilists, see rooted in Man's diversity stems not from human nature but from the presence in society of class conflict which stems from scarcity. There is therefore no need for conflicts of value to be perpetual (p.113).

The defensiveness that prompted Berlin to opt for a negative view of liberty is not needed once it is seen that the underpinning theory of human nature is erroneous. Once we conceive Man as a being who possesses capacities that will, when exercised, harmonise then our concern with liberty will be the positive one of seeking to remove obstacles to this exercise. This can be succintly illustrated by the debate on the connexion between the principles of liberty and private property. One argument is that private property supports an area of liberty that legitimately excludes others from interference. The other argument is that property constitutes an obstacle to the realisation of freedom. Which of these arguments is adopted will be affected by whether or not it is held that Man is perfectible or imperfectible. On the former reading of human nature there is no inherent justification for obstacles to freedom because left to their own devices in a suitable environment humans will not 'interfere' with each other. But on the latter reading these obstacles are better seen as bulwarks to freedom, because, on that reading, it is 'against human nature' to expect such harmony between human beings.

The aim of this schematic chapter has been to illustrate a variety of the ways in which human nature can be seen to matter in politics. If political disputes or arguments are analysed then certain assumptions about human nature will be uncovered. Similarly if the arguments of a particular theorist are analysed then certain assumptions about human nature will be found. The ubiquitous presence of these assumptions (though they themselves differ) is itself a point of some significance. What is also significant is that these assumptions are important ones. They play an effective and formative role in determining the character and shape of the arguments. What this chapter has not done is to enquire why the concept of human nature should enjoy this status of ubiquity and efficacy. Such an enquiry necessitates an examination of the concept itself and it is to that task that the remainder of this book is devoted. However, before embarking upon that task the nature of the enterprise needs to be clearly stated. In the following chapters I outline what I take to be involved in utilising the concept of human nature. This is not intended as a legislative exercise but as a task of explication. Accordingly, the discussion is properly conditional – *if* the notion of human nature is utilised then certain things follow.

2 Human Nature as a Practical Concept

'What is human nature?' is a conceptual question. It asks what is the appropriate language to employ when discussing human nature. It is the argument of this chapter explicitly, and of the following chapters implicitly, that human nature is a practical rather than a theoretical concept. This argument will be developed in three stages. The first preliminary stage explains the meaning of *'practice'*. The second stage supplies the crucial discussion by outlining the way in which the concept of human nature is a conceptual whole that possesses descriptive and prescriptive *duality*. The final stage provides examples of how this duality manifests itself in the ascription of an *ideal* character to human nature.

Theory and practice

The source of the distinction that I employ between theoretical and practical concepts is the philosophy of Aristotle. The dominant characteristic of Aristotle's philosophy is the analysis of the essential nature of things. This nature is discerned by discovering what the thing's function or purpose, its end (*telos*) is. According to Aristotle it is Man's essential nature to think or reason. The purpose of this reasoning, the purpose of Man's intellect, is to seek the truth. Humans, however, engage in two sorts of reasoning to attain two sorts of truth, namely, those of theory and those of practice (1976, Book 6).

The truths of theory constitute scientific knowledge (*episteme*). This knowledge is characterised by demonstrative necessity; it deals with those things which are eternal and invariable. Examples of

29

what Aristotle means by science are mathematics, physics and
metaphysics or theology. Mathematics studies unchanging
relationships like $2 + 2 = 4$; physics studies the unchanging
universal features of nature like the boiling point of liquids and
metaphysics studies the unchanging ground of all Being, the First
Cause.

The truths of practice constitute prudence (*phronesis*). Prudence
is characterised by deliberation or the weighing up of options; it
deals with those things which are variable – 'practical good is that
which is capable of being otherwise' (1967, p.291). Whilst science
thus aims simply at truth, prudence aims at truth that corresponds
with right desire (Hardie, 1968, p.224), that is, it concerns itself with
finding the true way or means by which to attain good ends. The
attainment of these ends is a matter of prudence not science because
we do not merely wish to know what courage is, but to be
courageous; we do not merely wish to know what justice is, but to be
just (1952, p.217). Courage and justice are practical goods, they
pertain to human action or practice (*praxis*). Prudence or practical
wisdom will thus concern itself with the sphere of human goods,
with what is 'capable of action with regard to the things that are
good or bad for man' (1976, p.209). Aristotle cites Pericles, the
leader of the Athenians in their war against Sparta, as an exemplary
exponent of that wisdom. Pericles is exemplary because he could
envisage what was good for both himself and for others.

As this citation of Pericles suggests, the study of politics, because
its purpose is 'the good for man', is, for Aristotle, the most eminent
representative of practical knowledge (1976, p.64). Understood in
this way politics is a branch of ethics. This is not to confine it
narrowly for 'ethics' here means not merely questions of personal
morality but the whole field of human institutions. This distinction
between the personal and the institutional is akin to that drawn by
Hegel (1942) between Morality and Ethical Life, where the latter
deals with domestic, economic, legal, historical as well as with
political and constitutional principles and institutions. As will
become clearer in this chapter it is this broad understanding of
politics with which this book is concerned.

The aim of this chapter is to explore the ramifications of locating
the concept of human nature within the ambit of practical intellect.
Though human nature is an item of practical philosophy it is so in a

distinctive way. This distinctiveness can be brought out initially – though not fully until all three facets have been examined – by elaborating uncritically upon this Aristotelian distinction between theory and practice. Geology is an example of science since its subject-matter operates independently of human choice. Geologists seek to understand, for example, earthquakes and the composition of rocks. While they may be motivated by a concern to protect human life or to exploit the earth's mineral resources for economic advantage, the understanding they achieve is a distinct matter from what motivated their enquiry or from any financial or other material benefit they may derive from it. This means that geology can have a conceivable raison d'être in the sheer 'theoretical' search into the nature of the earth's physical processes. By contrast, jurisprudence is a discipline whose subject-matter is constituted by human choices. Lawyers (in their various ways) seek to direct human life – did she steal? is that title good? is that a just law? was a contract completed? and so on. The very raison d'être of jurisprudence is determined by these 'practical' considerations.

It might appear from these examples that 'human nature' as a concept is more theoretical than it is practical. It could well be argued that just as the earth's crust and its 'history', with respect to its composition and processes, is independent of human volition so too is the nature of Man. Just as it is the business of the geologist to describe the earth and provide a record of the facts as to, say, the age of the Grampians, so human nature can equally be solely the object of descriptive and factual record. While it is indeed a facet of the concept of human nature that it establishes certain given limits (see Chapter 7), it is the crux of this chapter that the claim for the concept being solely descriptive is misconceived. In essence it is misconceived because it does not account adequately for the role that a concept of human nature plays. It does not, in other words, appreciate that the point of utilising the concept is a practical one. As the next section will elaborate, a conception of human nature is inseparable from a conception of what constitutes human life and activity. It is because politics is itself a human activity that human nature is a political issue. In Aristotelian parlance the answer to the question 'what is Man?' is inseparable from providing, if only implicitly, an answer to our key political question, 'what is the good for Man?'

Duality

The first step is to examine the nature of geological facts more
closely. Geologists make a three-fold classification of rocks into
igneous, sedimentary and metamorphic. To describe, as a matter of
fact, a particular rock as metamorphic is to subsume it within this
classification. It is by virtue of this classification that this fact is
established. Since this classification embodies concepts relating to
how rocks are formed it can be said that this fact is 'concept-laden'.
This is true of all 'facts' because the world does not describe itself,
does not present itself to us already labelled. We use concepts not
just in academic but also in everyday life. Hilary Putnam takes the
sentence 'the cat is on the mat' and points out how 'cat' reveals that
the distinction between animate and inanimate is judged to be
significant, how 'mat' reveals an interest in a distinction between
artifacts and non-artifacts within the category 'inanimate' and how
'on' is relevant because of our interest in spatial relations (1981,
pp.201–2). The notions of 'significance' and 'relevance' will occupy
us shortly. It is this unity of facts and concepts that is used to order
the world around us and since this ordering can be done for different
reasons so the 'facts' in question are relative and relevant to these
reasons. Thus the self-same object can be a rock to the layman, a
sample of gneiss to the geologist and a combination of atoms to the
physicist.

Around each fact there is, as it were, a penumbra, an implied
context. It is the presence of this context that makes most
statements of fact uncontentious. Just such a context is assumed by
Dahl when he gives as a quite deliberate example of an exclusively
factual assertion the proposition that 'Nixon won more popular
votes in the 1968 presidential election than Hubert Humphrey'
(1970a, p.104). This is only uncontentious because the meaning of
'votes', 'presidential', 'election' and even 'won' and '1968' are taken
for granted. (Pointing out this context does not of course detract in
any way from the palpability of the fact that Nixon did indeed beat
Humphrey.) It is equally the case that the 'facts' of human nature
will depend on a context.

Since all phenomena can be described or classified in an
indefinite number of ways (they are 'underdetermined') then to say
of some attributes that these are 'the facts of human nature' is
uninformative until we know what the conceptual context is.

Hence, parallel to the example of the rock in the last paragraph, Man can be considered to be a political animal to an Aristotelian; a sinner to a Christian; an independent rational agent to a Lockean; a creative communal worker to a Marxist; a product of genetic natural selection to a sociobiologist and so on and on. But while the physicist and the geologist cannot meaningfully be said to be in competition, we can, as we saw in Chapter 1, properly talk of the 'disagreement' between, say, Locke and Marx over the nature of Man. Why should there be this difference?

That question is best answered by posing another – what is the role or function, what is the point in having, a theory of human nature? This is the crucial question. The answer, and this is why practicality is a facet of the concept of human nature, is that the concept of human nature is an integral part of having a conception of the nature and character of human life and activity, of which politics is an intrinsic ingredient. I will refer to this as a conception of *human conduct* and I include in this term the entire institutional matrix of human life. (My usage is thus less restrictive than Oakeshott's (1975).) To propound a theory of human nature is to make certain claims about human conduct: this indeed is why recourse to 'human nature' is a political issue. Whereas the point of the geologist's classification/identification of facts can meaningfully be theoretical truth (*episteme*), the point of the classification/identification of facts about human nature is practical truth (*praxis*). Whereas to say that granite is a composite of quartz, mica and felspar leaves the world 'as found' (so to speak) because this fact could not 'be otherwise', to say that Man is a political animal makes, as we observed in Chapter 1, a profound difference as to what it is thought appropriate for human beings to do, for example, whether or not political apathy is a satisfactory form of life. It is, to repeat, this practical dimension that constitutes the point of having a concept of human nature in the first place.

We can best develop this argument by picking up a further aspect of the distinction between theory and practice. Human beings inhabit a world of natural objects such as granite, the annual cycle of the seasons, the combustibility of coal, the evaporation of water and so on. As befits their susceptibility to scientific knowledge (*episteme*) these objects exist or function independently of human action. Human beings, however, also inhabit a world of their own making – a human world. This world is comprised of such institutions and activities as politics, commerce, art, religion, law, sport and so on. To say these institutions are 'made' by humans does not entail that they are the purposive creations of specifiable individuals. Even if Webb Ellis originated rugby by picking up a soccer ball he did not intend to invent a new game. As befits their susceptibility to practical reason these institutions are capable of 'being otherwise' (think of the change from soccer to rugby). This capability is necessary so that there may be political action. That assertion merely depends on accepting, along the lines pursued in Chapter 1, that politics is inseparable from dispute. Once that is accepted then for there to be 'politics' there must be something to dispute – is commerce inimical to virtue? should heretics be compelled to come into the Church? In contrast to this the order of the natural world, whereby spring follows winter, operates regardless of human action. Of course, the explanation of this order may be disputed but such dispute is part of the human world; it forms, for example, an ineliminable role in that most human of institutions – the university. The significance of this distinction between the human and the natural worlds is, for our purposes, that the criterion implied in political activity is human action.

The immediate bearing (further aspects will be covered in Chapter 7) of the distinction between the natural and the human worlds is that the latter is constituted by human conduct. To participate in a barter, for example, implies that the participants know at minimum what each is doing and what, as a consequence, they are doing in concert. It is not necessary to a successful exchange that they know economic theory. Economic theory, however, has for its subject-matter human transactions. One factor necessary to account for these transactions is an account of the springs of human action. We can thus expect, in accord with our earlier comment that the concept of numan nature is integral to an understanding of human conduct, that an economic theory will have within it some concept of Man.

Adam Smith's theory satisfies this expectation. Smith remarked of the system of exchange that it was uniquely human for 'nobody ever saw a dog make a fair and deliberate exchange of one bone for another with another dog' (1976, p.26). Smith held accordingly that there was a propensity in human nature to truck, barter and exchange. To exchange is to seek to satisfy a want through mutual reciprocation – 'give me what I want and you shall have this which you want'. The propensity to exchange is thus implicitly the corollary of a conception of human nature which holds that humans seek primarily their own interest. The upshot is in a celebrated passage that 'it is not from the benevolence of the butcher, the brewer or the baker that we accept our dinner, but from their regard to their own interest. We address ourselves not to their humanity but to their self-love, and never talk to them of our necessities but of their advantages' (p.27).

This explanation of the relationship between a theory of human nature and economic activity does not leave the world as found. It establishes a context which accounts for an aspect of human conduct and which thereby also establishes what it is appropriate to do in economic transactions. In Smith's own case it so happened that this explanation was historically important. It became one of the resources that enabled 'men of commerce' to justify to themselves (and others) that to seek their own advantage was not reprehensible but was in accord with the facts of human nature (the full import of that final point will be brought out later in this chapter as well as in Chapter 7). But economics is a practical rather than a theoretical science and the facts 'could be otherwise'. Accordingly, and this is a point central to our argument, a different economic theory with a different account of the facts of human nature would establish a different context and a different ground for action in the human world. For Marx, for example, it would be in accord with the facts of human nature for wants to be satisfied as a direct expression of Man's communitarian nature without any need for some reciprocation (1975, pp.263–5).

We can say, therefore, that by not leaving matters as found a concept of Man establishes the ground for action in the world. We will develop this shortly but another example will serve to underline its meaning. If, as Burke said (see Chapter 1), Man is a religious animal, then it gives the place of religion in the world, and its bearing on human life, a different significance than, say, Freud's view (1960) that all religions have evolved out of a guilt-laden search for a substitute father-figure. While for Burke we should act to protect religion against misbegotten schemes to dispense with it, for Freud we should act to throw it off as a 'neurotic relic' (1964, p.72).

This example bears out further the difference between the natural and the human worlds. Geologists (now) possess an agreed context within which the facts of metamorphosis, for example, can be held to be established. But there is no such agreement regarding religion. This lack of agreement is inherent. Burke and Freud each hold the view that they do about religion because of their basic understanding of human nature *and* this understanding is integral to their conception of human conduct or their 'practical' appreciation of the institutions of the human world.

The concept of human nature provides a criterion for acting, or not acting, in the world. This means that the conceptual context within which the facts of human nature are identified is orientated towards practice. Such facts establish a context within which it is possible to identify what it is appropriate for humans to do (such as whether to cherish or abolish religion). This factual establishment of what is appropriate is thus also the establishment of a context of normative significance. However, there is here just one context. It is not so much a question of having the facts of human nature on the one side and the values or norms on the other but rather that the facts and values are best understood as dual elements, like the warp and weft of a fabric, that constitute a conceptual whole. The concept of human nature is, therefore, a whole that enjoys a duality; it is at once descriptive and prescriptive.

Two examples might help to clarify this duality. To say that Man is rational is to establish a particular context which does not merely identify a set of facts, such as speech or the ability to act against instincts (as in suicide), as significant but which also expresses a normative point of view. In one version this view might be that Man (unlike brutes) has a special relationship to God. Since the facts and the value constitute a whole then we can put this the other way round. It is the normative belief that Man is created in God's image that provides – in this version – the point behind the conceptual identification of rationality (absent in brutes for they can neither speak nor commit suicide) as a fact of human nature. By incorporating this normative belief the fact that Man is rational has prescriptive force, so that it is appropriate for Man to kill brutes but not other rational beings.

The second example is more specific. Rousseau declares it to be beyond dispute that humans, as individuals and as a species, uniquely possess the faculty of self-improvement (1962, p.48). This is a matter of fact (only humans mentally degenerate) but it is simultaneously an expression of value (the tyranny that Man now exercises over both himself and nature is a development and is thus not connate). Again this can be put the other way round. It is Rousseau's normative belief that Man is naturally or inherently good (p.100) which provides the point behind his making the capacity to develop a fact of human nature. This fact also licenses Rousseau to put down present misery to contingent external circumstances. Additionally it enables him consistently to write *The Social Contract* because in that book he envisages this factual capacity developing in a desirable direction.

Human nature thus possesses a descriptive and prescriptive duality. This means that when in political argument recourse is had to human nature, it is being claimed that the facts descriptively are so-and-so *and* that these facts prescriptively are significant or normatively authoritative for comprehending human conduct. The achievement of that comprehension provides the point behind holding some facts relevant and others not so.

Since these last remarks are important, we need to expand upon them. What for one theorist is a relevant and salient fact about human nature, for example, that Man alone has 46 chromosomes, could be for another theorist an irrelevance. The chromosome count would be irrelevant for this latter theorist because biological data do not enter into her conceptual classification. The classification is decisive because it determines what is to count as a description of human nature (cf. Casey, 1973, p.75). By not recognising the relevance of the description of human nature in terms of chromosomes then, in accord with the concept's wholeness, the normative authority implicit in a depiction of human nature is also denied. There is – and this is a key point – an important distinction to be made between statements that happen to refer to human beings and those that articulate a theory of human nature. These do not necessarily coincide. The former could well be an object of theoretical science whilst the latter, as we have argued, is a practical concept. To claim that the chromosome count is relevant to human nature is to place that fact in a practical context; it is to 'go beyond' a statement *about chromosomes* to one which relates to human conduct.

That 'relation' can only be made by providing reasons. In this case an argument must be supplied to connect genes and human action and institutions. We will consider such arguments in Chapter 7 but here it is enough to point out that the accuracy of the chromosome count need not be disputed; all that needs to be disputed is the relevance of selecting that fact, within a class of causes, to explain, for example, religion. The point here being made can be emphasised by noting that the facts that the human body consists of a particular mixture of gases and chemicals – hydrogen, oxygen, iron, calcium and so on – have never, so far as I know, been made the basis of a concept of human nature. Such facts occur in statements that happen to refer to human beings and not in theories of human nature because no reasons have been supplied to connect the human chemical constitution with human conduct.

The crucial issue is thus what is to count as a description of *human nature*. To develop this we can return to our two theorists. They might both accept that Man alone has 46 chromosomes, and agree that *that* is not a salient fact. They may adopt such a position because they judge it to be merely a question of numbers (*homo sapiens* has two fewer chromosomes than the chimpanzee). Since this fact is judged not to represent a qualitative difference then it does not belong in a theory of human nature. Accordingly nothing follows from the chromosome count as to what it is appropriate for humans to do because (for these two) this 'count' is a theoretical not a practical matter. But, to repeat, this is only so because chromosomes are judged not to be elements in a theory that claims to depict human nature.

This granted we can now attribute some further arguments to our two theorists. They both accept that Man speaks a specific native tongue but here one of them (Fichte for example) might regard this fact as salient whilst the other might put this into the same category as the chromosome count. What accounts for this difference is their different conceptual contexts. A dispute between them would in essence take the form of Fichte trying to make the other theorist attribute salience to the same facts as he does, that is, to adopt his context. Only by so doing could Fichte hope to persuade that theorist that this fact of human nature has some normative force – in this case that those who speak the same tongue constitute a nation which as such has the right to govern itself. The internal boundaries which are established by a shared tongue and which express in their diverse forms the nature of Man should determine the external political boundaries of states (Fichte, 1968, 12th. and 13th. Addresses). Since it is human nature that is deeply at issue then such differences have practical import.

We can illustrate this import with a concrete example. Marx

would fail to recognise as a relevant fact of human nature what for Augustine is salient, namely, human pride. To say that pride is salient for Augustine means it plays a prominent role in his conception of human conduct. Thus pride is the beginning of sin and it is sin which is 'the mother of servitude, the first cause of man's subjection of man' (1945, vol. 2, p.253). Since this is a given item of human nature, and thence beyond earthly remedy (see Chapter 7), then it is appropriate that servants obey their masters and 'serve them with cheerfulness and goodwill'. In contrast, while in no way denying that humans experience pride, Marx does not imbue it with similar significance and because of that he does not draw Augustine's conclusions as to what it is appropriate for subjects to do. The 'mother of servitude' for Marx is not human nature but social class. The class which controls a society's productive forces rules that class which lacks such control. That control, given certain earthly conditions (development in these productive forces), is remediable. Accordingly, Marx's injunction to the proletariat is revolution and, as such, is directly contrary to that issued by Augustine to servants.

There is one final aspect of this duality to broach. We observed at the end of Chapter 1, that the concept of human nature is both ubiquitous and efficacious. This observation reflects a commonplace in political theory. This commonplace is that (in Alan Ryan's version) 'an account of human nature is intrinsic to moral and political argument' (1973, p.3). Like many commonplaces this one is rarely subjected to examination and we shall explain in Chapter 10 why this sentiment is indeed expressed so frequently. However, our current task is to explore the link between duality and that intrinsicality to which Ryan refers.

This exploration can be conducted with the aid of the writings of Isaiah Berlin. Berlin declares that, 'the ideas of every philosopher concerned with human affairs in the end rests on his conception of what man is and can be' and he further holds that this 'central notion or image' since it 'determines their picture of the world' is more important than the arguments employed to defend their views and confute objections to them (1981, p.298). Since this determining conception of Man is indeed so central, it follows that

'to think of someone as a human being is *ipso facto* to bring into play notions like "society, freedom, sense of time and change, suffering, happiness, productivity, good and bad, choice, effort,

truth, illusion" so that to say of someone he is a man, but that
choice or the notion of truth, mean nothing to him would be
eccentric: it would clash with what we mean by "man" . . . as
intrinsic to the way we think and (as a matter of brute fact)
evidently cannot but think.' (1967, pp.26–7)

This 'bruteness' is itself a truth of 'human nature' and explains
why the concept of Man can never be a mere descriptive term. In
studying human nature we are studying ourselves. This identity of
studied (object) and studier (subject) is another reason why
knowledge of human nature does not leave the world 'as found'.
Because of this identity of studier and studied a description of
human nature is always in some measure a self-description. But a
self-description is no neutral datum. Burke's religious beliefs, for
example, were not something separable or detachable from his own
sense of who he was and his conviction that Man was a religious
animal reinforced his belief and informed his understanding of
human conduct. Berlin echoes this when he generalises that humans
'choose as they do, because their life and thought are determined by
fundamental moral categories and concepts that are . . . a part of
their being and thought and sense of their own identity; part of what
makes them human' (1969, pp.171–2).

Nietzsche provides a dramatic exemplification of this. Nietzsche
accepted the message of Darwin's thesis that Man is an animal but
he denied the usual nineteenth-century gloss that this therefore
gives Man, as the most evolved species, a superiority. For
Nietzsche evolution truly has no purpose; Man is not the product of
a special design (1968a, p.54). This is the meaning of Nietzsche's
frequent declarations that God is dead. Knowing this, where does it
leave him (and us)? One consequence is that the much vaunted
truths of logic are no more than biological compulsions and,
relatedly, that language, the vehicle of thought, is itself mere
prejudice (1968b, pp.278, 283). Acting on this knowledge Nietzsche
deliberately wrote unsystematically – using aphorisms, puns and
poetic imagery (not for nothing did he call one of his works *The
Jovial Science*). A second consequence is that all the old values, like
charity, generosity, humility and their modern counterparts like
equality and democracy, which are based on the idea of Man as a
product of design, should be surmounted. Nietzsche accordingly set
himself up with deliberate provocation as an 'immoralist' (1933,

p.59) and he baited Christianity ceaselessly as the prime embodiment of an insipid 'slave morality', a morality that equated goodness with stupidity (1907, p.231).

What Nietzsche exemplifies is that our humanity is not a matter of indifference to us. The crucial factor is how we construe this humanity: we are religious, political, the products of natural selection and so on. To avoid a possible misunderstanding it perhaps needs to be observed that to deny that our humanity is a matter of indifference does *not* mean that self-preservation is necessarily the major value. The Stoics, as we shall note in more detail in Chapter 4, held life itself, to be a matter of indifference. What matters to the Stoic was the sort of life we live and if we are forced into having to lead an unworthy, inappropriate, life then we are obliged to commit suicide. Alternatively, in 'heroic' cultures, like that portrayed by Homer, it is better, more appropriate, to die (gloriously) in battle than it is to flee and live (ignobly). Both the Stoic sage and the Homeric hero have an understanding of the nature of Man, which supplies them with a model or ideal which as such recommends to them what are appropriate actions to undertake. We are thus back to the duality of human nature and how, to cite C. B. Macpherson, 'the very structure of our thought and language puts an evaluative content into our descriptive statements about "man" ' (1973, p.53).

Ideality

This section develops the notion that a standard or an ideal is implicit in the identification of a set of characteristics as definitive of human nature. To establish what is human nature is also to establish what it is for Man to live well. There are two major ways in which the idea of human nature can serve as an ideal.

The first of these is that to identify a human institution or activity as contrary to human nature is to appraise it negatively. For example, for the young Marx a society based purely on exchange or credit alienates Man from the true productive species essence. This notion of alienation only has meaning when set alongside an implied ideal condition of unalienated life. This life is that which humans ought to live and is that wherein human nature is truly exhibited. In line with the concept's duality this is not put forward by Marx as a mere value-choice but as a true statement of the facts of the matter relative to human nature. Though obscured and distorted by the perverse demands of capitalism the relationship of, for example, man to woman is an 'observable fact' that reveals the extent to which Man's 'human nature has become nature for him . . . the extent to which in his most individual existence he is at the same time a communal being' (1975, p.347). In similar fashion patriarchalism of the Filmerian variety is unacceptable to Locke because it is incompatible with the equality, liberty and independence which are definitive of 'the natural condition of mankind'.

It is in this way, as noted above, that a concept of human nature provides a ground for action in the human world. Accordingly, Hobbes would say that a Godwinian-type anarchism is bound to fail. This failure is directly attributable to such a social arrangement running counter to the nature of Man. It is in the nature of (Hobbesian) Man to do and not be done by (the 'laws' of Nature are 'contrary to our natural passions' (1914, p.87)). The effect of this is to destabilise the possibility of reciprocity in human relationships that is presumed by Godwinian teaching. Hobbes is then able to say because of this instability generated by human nature that governance is *necessary* in human relationships. As we shall note in detail in Chapter 7, this same argument is used in contemporary biological theorising about human nature. Hence when E. O. Wilson declares anarchism to be 'impossible' (1978, p.208) he is revealing, despite his conviction that he is putting forward an objective, scientific account of human nature, that he too possesses some ideal as to how human life has to be led. He knows negatively that it is inappropriate to live (or attempt to live) anarchistically, that would not be to live well.

The second manifestation of this ideality is the positive side of the same coin. Human nature is made manifest when Man is all that he or she can be, all that he or she essentially is. We have already noted in passing the role of the sage in Stoicism and the hero in the Homeric epic and similar roles are played by, amongst others, the pious in Christian thought and the autonomous independent agent of liberalism. We can elucidate the reasoning behind this positive ideality by examining Aristotle's case for the contemplative life.

As we remarked earlier, it is definitive of the Aristotelian enterprise that the criterion of being a 'man' is inseparable from the criterion for being a 'good man' (somewhat in the same way that the criterion of a knife is that it cuts cleanly). In his *Nicomachean Ethics* (book 1, chapter 7) Aristotle asks the question 'what is the function or end of man?' Since life as such is enjoyed by plants as well as animals then that does not serve to identify what is distinctively human. This same imprecision rules out sentience, since that does not distinguish Man from animals. What remains is thought or reason, so that the proper function of Man is 'a kind of life, namely, an activity or series of actions of the soul, implying a rational principle' (1976, p.76).

Human beings, however, are capable of leading three sorts of life – the pleasurable, the political and the contemplative (p.68). The first of these is little more than animalistic and those who pursue it are servile. The end (*telos*) of the political life is said here to be honour. A life of honour, however, lacks self-sufficiency because it is dependent on others to bestow or withhold. The most complete or self-sufficient life is that most in conformity with Man's proper nature (reason) and this is the life of contemplation (the pursuit of theoretical truth). As the intellect is the highest 'thing' in us then contemplation is the highest activity (p.331). Whereas other human activities, such as labour or politics, are done for the sake of something other than themselves (such as satisfaction of needs or attainment of honour) contemplation is alone done for its own sake. The objects of theoretical knowledge are eternal, they cannot be changed by human action. The contemplative life as the most complete life is also the most fulfilling. Aristotle takes it as axiomatic that Man desires happiness. This 'happiness' should not be confused with the pursuit of pleasure (hedonism) which is the mere satisfaction of appetites and which is, as such, a transient, subjective state or condition. 'Happiness' rather is 'virtually a kind of good life or prosperity' (p.78) whereby men flourish by doing successfully those actions wherein they fulfil themselves as men. It follows that if the contemplative life is the most distinctively human then that life will also be the happiest.

As in the negative argument, there is in the positive argument an implied view of society where truly human society is exhibited. Thus C. B. Macpherson produces a list of essential human attributes, 'the capacity for rational understanding, for moral judgment and action, for aesthetic creation and contemplation, for the emotional activities of friendship and love, and sometimes for religious experience' (1973, p.4). These 'capacities' (see Chapter 8) require for their fulfilment a democratic society but such a society cannot be a capitalist market one because in that society men and women do not develop their capacities and thus fail to live as fully human a life as is possible (1973, p.51).

The basic point can be illustrated by a very different and final example. The key feature of human nature as portrayed by the Romantic movement was that Man uniquely possessed a creative imagination. The ideal Man is the artist or the poet (it was of the essence of Shelley's defence of poetry (1970) that poets were the true legislators of the world). The poet is one who 'sees' the world in a unique way and in so doing displaces expectations and conventions so that others too come to see the world differently. Whilst countless numbers have seen daffodils growing profusely or heard nightingales sing it takes a Wordsworth or a Keats not only to encapsulate the primitive delight that such vistas and sounds afford but also to appreciate nature anew, to enrich our experience and enable us to see with more than what Blake termed our 'corporeal eye'.

Since we are ideally creatures of imagination, we should not passively accept received wisdom nor routinely conform to established practices but should cast off our inhibitions and commonplaces. Each should aspire to live an authentic life and since each and every individual is their own source of standards, actions which are merely conventional have of themselves no imperative weight. Simply to follow rules or customs (to imitate) is to abrogate one's humanity. This humanity is expressed in our individuality not in our common characteristics. There is a sense in which this concentration on self betrays an unpolitical frame of mind (which, of course, is itself a political stance) but such a judgment would be unjust. Many of the earliest critics of industrial society were, in their diverse ways, subscribers to an essentially Romantic outlook. In part this is because of the presence of a strong anti-modernist ingredient in that outlook but their ideal of human nature led these Romantics to criticise modern industrial society, with its dull, repetitive ('soul destroying') routines, for preventing individuals from living an authentic life. Colmer's remark on Coleridge holds good more generally, 'whatever tended to debase the nobility of human nature whether it was slavery, the employment of young children in the cotton mills or the acceptance on the part of the commercial classes of Malthusian economic doctrine, became an object of bitter attack' (1959, p. 179).

Finally we can observe that because a theory of human nature incorporates an ideal within it then recourse to a concept of human nature is not necessarily supportive of an existing status quo. The idea that 'human nature' can be used as a critical tool will be met again in Chapter 8.

3 Facts, Values and Human Nature

The aim of this chapter is to trace some of the implications of the argument developed in Chapter 2. In particular, the idea of the duality of the concept of human nature needs pursuing further. If, as the idea of duality indicates, the concept commingles description and prescription then it might imply the utility of the concept is suspect. The chief cause of this suspicion is that the concept combines what are, or what should be, separate ingredients – usually referred to as facts and values. This is a large issue and we cannot hope to examine it in all its ramifications here. But there are two contrasting implications that we can take up not merely for their own sake but also because we will further advance in so doing the argument of Chapter 2. The first implication is that the notion of human nature has no place in the scientific study of politics, whereas the second implication is that a notion of human nature is an integral component in attaining a true understanding of politics. As we shall see the key source of this contrast is the way in which the relationship between facts and values is understood.

Human nature and political science

The relationship between facts and values can be set out in the form of a dilemma. If, on the one hand, human nature is a matter of factual description (what *is* the case) then as such it cannot prescribe (what *ought* to be the case). Anthony Quinton states this position clearly, 'the nature of men is the set of defining characteristics in virtue of having which things are identified as being men. These characteristics are in fact empirical and so no conclusion about what men ought to be allowed can be extricated from the concept itself'

(1967, p.8). To think otherwise is to commit the 'naturalistic fallacy' (see pp.50–1, below).

If, on the other hand, statements about human nature are making value-judgments then these statements, because they are either matters of personal opinion or are emotional responses that are inescapably subjective in meaning, cannot be objective matters of factual record. Value-judgments thus cannot form the subject-matter of science – witness their absense in geology. If, as Chapter 2 maintained, the concept of human nature possesses prescriptive/descriptive duality then the concept appears to have no place in political science.

Political science here means an attempt to provide testable generalisations. What makes phenomena testable is their amenability to objective observation and thus to measurement and quantification. This was why Dahl's example, given above, of an exclusively factual assertion, referred to votes cast. The counting of votes is a matter of enumeration. Numbers cannot lie and they can thus command the acceptance of rival candidates; the political values of the candidates cannot affect the rules of arithmetic. The achievement of scientific status thus depends on confining the field of political science to what is, in principle, susceptible to objective assessment. To achieve this goal, to aspire to the status of a theoretical science like geology, all value-terms must be eradicated. We can illustrate this ideal by the arguments of Felix Oppenheim (1973).

Oppenheim is a careful, sophisticated and non-extreme proponent of the need for the study of politics to be scientific and he holds that this goal can be achieved by explicating basic concepts in terms acceptable to all, that is, regardless of normative or ideological commitments. This will be achieved by making the validity of statements containing these concepts depend 'exclusively on intersubjectively ascertainable empirical evidence' (p.56). We can appreciate his meaning from an example gleaned from his own positive writings: 'The existence of a freedom relationship depends entirely on empirical facts, not on the speaker's normative views about liberty, and not even on the preferences of the actors between whom the relationship is said to hold' (1961, p.118). Rather than query this example we can simply ask what 'empirical facts' are relevant to Augustine's and Marx's accounts of human nature? Both might accept that human history is, as a matter of factual record, a record of inhumanity, but what basic concepts, what formulation of human nature, would they agree upon? A negative similarity – neither, for example, accepts a Hobbesian account – is insufficient and to assess their theories via another account, say Wilson's sociobiological one (see Chapter 7), is irrelevant, for why should Augustine or Marx accept an account of human nature (as opposed to a statement that happens to refer to human beings) couched in terms of genetic fitness? There is in this sense no neutral ground on which to stand. As Alasdair MacIntyre puts it, each form of social and moral practice 'carries with it its own picture of human nature' (1967, p.268). Augustine is never going to recognise an account of human nature that omits Man's sinfulness nor is Marx going to recognise an account that thinks altruism is not possible.

However attempts have been made to use 'human nature' in political science. The prime motivation behind these attempts is to 'get political philosophy out of the fact-free vacuum in which it had been contemplating human nature' (Knutson, 1972, p.3). We must, in other words, purge the concept of its prescriptivity and replace – for clearly facts and values are here assumed to be mutually exclusive – that with the facts of the matter. A noteworthy ('pathbreaking' (Schwartz, 1976, p.25)) example of these attempts is that of James Davies (1973).

In pursuing his line of enquiry Davies has, like many 'political scientists', had to accept observable behaviour as his starting point. Hence he formulates his key question as 'whether there are any basic behavioural tendencies common to all human beings that become manifest in politics' (p.3). This leads him to a Schumpeterian view of politics (see Chapter 1) where the elite 'present ends-and-means alternatives to the general public who in turn choose among the various alternatives presented to them by the elite' (p.24). More generally, and this is an aspect of his work to which we shall return in Chapter 5, Davies seeks to establish connexions between deprivation of physical needs and political apathy. Thus, according to Davies, individuals when not physically deprived will fulfil their 'self-realisation' needs in non-political channels and only become involved in political activity when governments impinge threateningly upon them. Active involvement in politics, it also follows, is the prerogative of only those few who enjoy it for its own sake (p.61).

However, as the discussion of democratic theory in Chapter 1 illustrated, Davies's approach and conclusions, though conforming to Oppenheim's recommendations, would fail to find universal acceptance. Pateman and Bachrach, for example, would see in this account a false apolitical reading of human nature. This means that without needing in any way to doubt Davies's factual material they would not give the facts that Davies adduces in support of his argument the same significance that he allots to them. Indeed, they would see his argument as upholding an elitist theory of democracy by attempting to give it the spurious (because methodologically unsound) support of scientific fact. (Chapter 7 will comment further on this alleged role of science.) But even if Pateman's and Bachrach's position is not accepted their response indicates that Davies, despite his pretensions to the contrary, has not succeeded in purging the concept of its duality. This is because the point of his enterprise is inseparable from placing political activity within a context of practical significance. We can discern his point in the facts that he holds to be salient and it is practically significant that universal involvement in politics cannot be rationally expected. Equally, of course, the point behind Pateman's and Bachrach's endeavours – their identification of salient facts – is to comprehend an aspect of human conduct. The facts of human nature (their conceptual context) in each case 'could be otherwise'. When considering human nature political science is a practical rather than a theoretical science.

What are the consequences of this conclusion? They could be either that it demonstrates that the notion of human nature should be dropped from political science or, conversely, that it demonstrates a fundamental inadequacy in this conception of political science. If however human nature is as central a notion as was maintained in Chapter 2, then it would seem to follow that the latter alternative is the more defensible conclusion to draw. As has been frequently pointed out (e.g. Wolin, 1972) to think that numerate precision (or statistical significance) is coterminous with the 'truth' of politics is a delusion (that is not to say it is useless). To give a stark, and hence perhaps unfair, example: to exclude the question of the meaning and character of a 'just society' from the study of politics, because this is an inescapably evaluative (that is non-scientific) conception is to throw the baby out with the bathwater. It is precisely because the question of justice (and the like) are disputed that there are any phenomena to study 'scientifically' in the first place.

If this is accepted then we need to find another, less restrictive, way of understanding politics. One such way is provided by an Aristotelian account. As identified at the outset of Chapter 2 this account is clear that politics is a 'practical' study. Crucially, and of course not accidentally, the concept of human nature plays a central role in that account. Given that this is the case then what does it entail with respect to the relationship between facts and values? To answer this question is to consider the second of the two implications identified above.

Human nature and political understanding

From this Aristotelian perspective, the dilemma set out above can be seen to be misleading for, as MacIntyre observes, Aristotle's arguments in the *Ethics* presuppose that the naturalistic fallacy is not a fallacy at all (1981, p.139). The dilemma hinges on the separation of facts from values. There is, however, a tradition of thought, that is largely Aristotelian in provenance, which does not accept that facts and values have to be divorced in the way the dilemma presents it. This tradition is represented by the doctrine known as 'ethical naturalism'. What is significant about this doctrine, and what makes it apposite to our purposes, is the role played within it by the concept of human nature. We can now examine this role. It should be emphasised that it is this role that is the focus of our interest and it is beyond our current brief to pronounce definitively on the nature of moral judgment. We can best commence by setting out the fallacy that this Aristotelian view of politics, as represented by ethical naturalism, is held to commit.

The term 'naturalistic fallacy' was coined by G. E. Moore and defined by him as the 'contention that good *means* nothing but some simple or complex notion that can be defined in terms of natural qualities' (1962, p.73: my emphasis). According to Moore goodness was indefinable and it was always, in consequence, fallacious to attempt to define it. With respect to what is propounded as a definition it is always possible to ask of what is propounded whether it is good – so, if *A* is good is the same as *A* is what is desired, it is still possible to ask 'is it good to desire *A*' (p.15). Considerable refinements have been made to Moore's argument so that while R. M. Hare, for example, finds the term 'naturalism' in Moore's use 'unfortunate' and the formulation of his argument to be 'at fault' yet Moore's critical argument is 'valid' and rests 'albeit insecurely upon a secure foundation' (1961, pp.82–3). Hare indeed develops a test akin to Moore's 'my argument is that we cannot say "x is a good A" *means* the same as "x is a A which is C", because then it becomes impossible to commend A's which are C by saying "A's which are C are good A's"' (p.89: my emphasis). As the wording here suggests the nub of Hare's account of the distinction between description and evaluation is that 'value-terms have a special function in language, that of commending; and so they plainly cannot be defined in terms of other words which themselves do not perform this function' (p.91). More simply, since it 'must be part of the function of a moral judgment to prescribe or guide choices . . . then it is clear . . . that no moral judgment can be a pure statement of fact' (p. 29).

   Though it is definitive of Hare's enterprise that there be this conceptual separation between description and evaluation yet he is able to maintain that 'almost every word in our language is capable of being used on occasion as a value-word' (p.79). He cites as an example the word 'brilliant' and later gives 'tidy' and 'industrious'. The last two are examples of words whose evaluative meaning is secondary to their descriptive meaning whereas, in contrast, with the word 'good' this order is reversed with the evaluative meaning assuming priority. Hare allows that moral terms do have descriptive meaning (1963, p.21), but denies that this is sufficient – there must be a prescriptive element. He believes that naturalists can only arrive at prescriptions if they camouflage an evaluative word as a descriptive word. As examples of this practice he supplies the word 'natural' and 'normal' (1961, p.92). These terms are 'covertly evaluative' and Hare believes that nearly all so-called 'naturalistic definitions' will break down when tested against the criterion that 'to be genuinely naturalistic a definition must contain no expression for whose applicability there is not a definite criterion which does not involve the making of a value-judgment' (1961, p.92).

   Given this how does Hare see the connexion between prescription and description occurring? The answer is by making a decision. Making a decision is for Hare 'the very essence of morals' (1961, p.54). Nothing in the use of words or in our psychological states can determine what is our duty; that determination can only follow from 'making a moral decision' (1961, p.44) because 'in the end everything rests upon such a decision of principle' (1961, p.69). In contrast to this (though see some later comments by Hare that perhaps mitigate the contrast, 1963, p.97, 195) what is characteristic of the Aristotelian ethical naturalist tradition is that prescription and description are linked through an understanding of human nature.

There are two issues involved in this linkage – one procedural (so to speak) the other substantive. The procedural issue hinges on the deliberate use of 'linkage' as a 'weasel word'. Hare's argument (though again there have been some shifts in it), as is Moore's, is an argument about meaning and logic. To them naturalism is untenable because they interpret it as a doctrine of entailment so that good *means* the same as or is *entailed* by pleasure (or whatever other fact is proposed). But that is not how naturalists see it (or at least how they need to see it). That is, though there is genuine dispute about the logical form of valid arguments in ethics, naturalists tend not to feel themselves tied to that dispute.

To exemplify the procedural issue we can cite Stuart Hampshire, who implicitly turns the tables by labelling it a fallacy to assume all argument is deductive. His own position is that 'in general one kind of sentence may be established and defended exclusively by reference to another kind, without the first kind being deducible, or logically derivable, from the second' (1972, p.51). This applies to the connexion between statements about physical things and statements about sensations. It also applies to the connexion between statements of people's character and statements about their behaviour. Accordingly, it follows that:

'we may properly elucidate moral or practical judgments by saying that they are established and supported by arguments consisting of factual judgments of a particular range, while admitting that they are never strictly deducible or in this sense logically derivable, from any set of factual judgments.' (1972, p.51)

Hampshire's point with regard to procedure can be developed by moving to the second, substantive, issue because it is through an interpretation of human nature that Hampshire's 'elucidation' proceeds. Charles Taylor agrees that it is a misplaced emphasis to fasten onto *meaning*. The claim (he continues) is not that 'good' means 'conducive to the fulfilment of human wants, needs and purposes' but that its use is 'unintelligible' outside of any relationship to these wants etc. (1973, p.167). The commendatory, prescribing, evaluating use of 'good' derives from human nature or, as Taylor less directly puts it, from use by a 'race of beings who are such that through their needs, desires and so on they are not indifferent to the various outcomes of the world-process. A race of inactive, godless angels, as really disinterested spectators would have no use for it [good]' (p.168). It is to Taylor a 'fact' that human beings are not indifferent.

This sort of substantive argument can of course be disputed and much hinges on the grounds of this disputation. In many ways the standard criticism of ethical naturalism is to provide counter-examples – not everybody, for example, thinks happiness and goodness are linked. More generally, ethical naturalism is held to be flawed because it cannot generate any definitive account of what is the good life for Man. This is not only because of the great variety of conceptions of the good life that have been held but also because, as John Cottingham expresses it, 'any feature or activity proposed as definitive of the nature or essence of man can be denied by a human agent in the sense that it is open to him to conduct his life without reference to that feature or activity' (1983, p.465). This point as Cottingham goes on to remark is at the heart of existentialism. (We shall deal with the existentialists' challenge to the concept of human nature in Chapter 9).

It is because the candidates for the *content* of morality are disputable that Hare sees the criteria of moral reasoning to lie in the *formal* characteristics of prescriptivity and universality,

> 'when we are trying in a concrete case to decide what we ought to do what we are looking for . . . is an action to which we can commit ourselves (prescriptivity) but which we are at the same time prepared to accept as exemplifying a principle of action to be prescribed for others in like circumstances (universalizability).' (1963, pp.89–90)

The thrust here is that these rules of moral reasoning are ethically neutral. They do not commit the reasoner to any particular moral opinion. This has the effect of making the link between facts and values contingent. No particular configuration of facts can license any particular set of values; we are always free to choose or decide. For example, the factually demonstrable redistributive effects of progressive rates of income tax are consistent with a judgment either that the rates be lessened or that they be heightened. In contrast to this – and here we come to the nub of the importance of this debate for our concerns – what a theory of human nature serves to do, within this Aristotelian tradition, is provide a ground for denying such contingency. It does this by claiming that in virtue of the nature of Man there is an unavoidable structure to what humans do and what they value. (As we shall see in Chapter 5 this argument also serves to rebut relativism.) Due to this structure there is a non-contingent character to the forms of human existence and hence there are limits to the factors that can be adduced in support of moral judgment (Williams, 1976, p.75). This connexion between 'limits' and human nature will form the staple ingredient of Chapter 7, but here two clarificatory points should be made. First this is without prejudice to the question that human existence itself might well be a contingent matter. Second, and more significantly, it is no real objection to this position to invoke scientific fiction. Putnam puts well the limitations of such invocations when he remarks:

> 'If there are beings on, say, Alpha Centauri, who cannot feel pain and who do not mind individual death, then very likely our fuss about "murder and suffering" will seem to them to be much ado about nothing. But the very alienness of such a life form means that they cannot understand the moral issues involved. If our "objectivity" is objectivity humanly speaking, it is still objectivity enough.' (1981, p.168)

This idea of non-contingency can be pursued a little further through a continued elaboration of ethical naturalism. It is the bedrock of ethical naturalism that moral argument and recommendation cannot be self-grounding in individual decision. This position is the main thrust in a well-known paper by Philippa Foot. Foot seeks to show in rebuttal of Hare that there are some things which do, and others which do not, count in favour of a moral conclusion and that 'a man can no more decide for himself what is evidence for rightness and wrongness than he can decide what is evidence of monetary inflation or a tumour on the brain' (1978, p.99). Giving the example of 'rudeness' she claims that, once the acceptability of that vocabulary has been established, the term has a proper application so that 'it follows that a man cannot make his own personal decision about the considerations which are to count as evidence in morals' (p.106). To Foot it seems 'undeniable' that moral concepts like rightness, obligation and duty are related to concepts of harm, advantage and importance. This argument is reiterated by, for example, Mary Midgley when she comments that it does 'not make sense' that moral notions could be blank contingencies (1980, p.216); moral vocabulary is related to the wants and needs of living beings, of 'more particularly human beings' (p.220). Both Foot and Midgley do of course, and typically, concede that these relationships are not straightforward and that they do require patient investigation.

What this investigation would show is the non-arbitrary, non-self-grounding, quality of moral judgment. The source of this non-arbitrariness is human nature. It is just to this non-arbitrary sense of 'nature' the ethical naturalist need apply (Monro, 1967, p.121). There is no need, that is to say, to be committed to the claim ' "x exists" therefore "x ought to exist" '. Nature is not being utilised as an external standard to afford some criterion of what we should do. In that guise it would indeed be open to J. S. Mill's criticism that,

> 'either it is right that we should kill because nature kills; torture because nature tortures; ruin and devastate because nature does the like; or we ought not to consider at all what nature does, but what it is good to do. If there is such a thing as a reductio ad absurdum, this surely amounts to one.' (1904, p.18)

To hold to a concept of human nature is to hold that human beings have a nature and by virtue of this nature there are certain types of activity that are satisfactory to them. Accordingly humans do what they do because they are what they are. Mill himself attests to this in a passage that G. E. Moore's criticism has made notorious, to wit, 'the sole evidence it is possible to provide that anything is desirable, is that people do actually desire it' (1972, p.32). In other words, it is senseless to regard as desirable something that is outside the human experience of a desired object, just as (to give one of Foot's examples) it would not make sense to regard clasping hands three times in an hour as a good action (p.118).

Human nature is the 'stuff' of morality and to ignore this by, like Hare, confining morality to formal principles is, from the naturalist perspective, to miss the very point of morality. Moral rules to be *moral* rules must impinge on something that *matters*, on something important and not trivial. What is deemed important must have some bearing on human interests (Hampshire, 1965, p.259). Even if, with Calvin, Man as such is held to be without value because all that is valuable emanates from God, still what is important is the proper human response to God, to wit, to live a Christian life of sobriety, righteousness and godliness (1953, vol. 2, p.9). These three then constitute the human virtues and the substance of human morality: to live a lustful, self-willed and impious life is to live a worse life than one committed to God. Hence even in this unpromising case Geoffrey Warnock's defence of a core content to morality will still hold. Warnock asks rhetorically

'is it not natural and besides a perfectly defensible position to reserve the appellation *moral* ideals for those whose pursuit is supposed to tend actually to do good rather than harm, to make things on the whole better rather than worse, while regarding as not forming part of any moral point of view such ideals as are openly destructive, or damaging or pointless or insane?' (1967, p.59: Warnock's emphasis)

There is a further point to be gleaned from Warnock's wording. He indicates that there is a 'natural' connexion between accepting a set of empirical premises (what actually does harm) and the acceptance of a normative conclusion (morality). The source of this 'naturalness' is the nature of Man. The obverse of this is that it would be 'unnatural' or perverse not to link morality with human well-being. Yet it is possible to be perverse. It is this possibility that is exploited by Hare and the other anti-naturalists. Since the connexion between morality and human well-being is not a *logical* doctrine of strict entailment then Hare and the others are perfectly well able to insist that there is no necessity here – it is always possible to refrain from accepting the evaluation (Hare, 1963, pp.189–90). It is, however, perhaps worth observing in conclusion that there is a sense in which this possibility is parasitic upon a naturalist foundation. Hume (the supposed begetter of the is/ought dichotomy) in fact provides an illustration of this point. Hume rejects the view of 'politicians' (he has Hobbes and Mandeville in mind) who would 'extirpate all sense of virtue from mankind' because it is impossible that artifice 'should be the sole cause of the distinction we make betwixt virtue and vice. For if nature did not aid us in this particular 'twould be in vain for politicians to talk of honourable and dishonourable, praiseworthy or blameable . . . nature must furnish the materials and give us some notion of moral distinctions' (1888, p.500).

Where does this leave us? We identified two implications of the view that human nature as a practical concept possesses a prescriptive and descriptive duality. On the first implication human nature could have a place in political science only if it was a descriptive notion. The practical character of the concept, however, served to make this restriction untenable. But this does not necessarily warrant the conclusion that the concept is therefore useless, rather it provides a reason for wanting a more inclusive approach to the study of politics. The second implication concerned how in an alternative Aristotelian view of politics the notion of human nature was central precisely in virtue of its duality. On this naturalist view values are valued as values by men and women as expressions of their constitutive humanity. A theory of human nature claims this constitutive humanity to be the fact of the matter. But, of course, the context that establishes what are the relevant facts of the matter is disputable. This disputability stems in essence from the fact that to evoke the notion of human nature is to make, at least implicitly, certain claims about human conduct and these, as practical truths, could be otherwise.

4 Human Nature as a Universal Concept

To believe in human nature is to believe that humankind possess some common attributes. These attributes are to be understood not as 'optional extras' but as belonging to Man as Man. They are universals in the sense that whenever and wherever humans are encountered these attributes also will be found. This view of commonality or universality does not claim that all humans are identical. Indeed, much of the purpose behind identifying universal attributes stems from the recognition that there are differences among humankind. The essential claim is therefore that these differences to not destroy universality but overlay it. Obvious difficulties now present themselves – how do we know if a particular attribute is universal or local? Is there a perspective which enables us to make that distinction? And if there is a doubt between the universal and the local in one case might not all cases be similarly affected so that there is here no meaningful distinction? And if there is no meaningful distinction then perhaps the very idea of distinguishing between 'common' and 'optional' attributes is a mistake?

These questions raise important political points. If all we can say universally about humans is that, for instance, they possess ear lobes (this example is Hegel's (1892, p.309)) then 'human nature' is not going to provide any political purchase. In terms of our discussion in Chapter 2, because the facet of practicality is absent there will be no theory of human nature, merely statements that happen to refer to humans. The significant implication of this is that the claimed for universality of human nature must have some bearing on human conduct.

To bring out the facet of universalism is the task of this and the two following chapters. This chapter picks out an important and

58

influential strand in the history of political thought. Chapter 5 will examine the challenges that have been and are made to universalism, as well as the ripostes to these. Chapter 6 will, in the light of these two chapters, examine three contemporary writers who devote explicit attention to the universality of human nature. By dealing with modern universalist political theory, Chapter 6 will complement the traditional understanding to be explored in this chapter.

To illustrate this traditional understanding I have chosen the Natural Law strand in the history of political thought. The point behind choosing this strand is intended to be more than merely illustrative. It is also intended to indicate that, through the frequent and persistent recourse to universalism which this history reveals, the universality of human nature is no merely subsidiary or optional aspect of political theory. This indication is indeed to be expected in the light of the commonplace, which we discussed in Chapter 2, to the effect that the notion of Man was central or intrinsic to any political theory. Though the history that we shall cursorily sketch is that of Western speculation the persistence of universalist claims about human nature is not confined to the West. For example, both of the two major traditions of ancient Chinese thought saw Man universally. In Confucian thought all humans possess, as well as behavioural constancies like eating and sleeping, certain social attributes like respectfulness, and most distinctively, as humans they possess an evaluative mind. Taoism rejected this latter aspect but placed paramount importance on each and every humans' possession, within themselves, of the timeless principle of *te*, which alone constituted their essential nature (Monro, 1969). Similarly it is a key element in both Buddhism and Jainism that, regardless of caste, sex or creed, everyone is capable of self-realisation (Raju, 1960).

We remarked in the opening paragraph to this chapter that the recognition of universality is related to the recognition of diversity. In Western thought this relationship first came into political prominence in the writings of the Greek Sophists and in the responses made to them by Plato and Aristotle. The Sophists were teachers and what they taught was how to be successful in the polis. Success depended on conforming to the prevailing customs. However, as the Greeks were well aware, customs differed between one polis and another. A consequence of this was that the criterion of success also differed, so that what might constitute success in one polis may well be unsuccessful in another. Generalised this meant that virtue was a matter of local social convention (*nomos*). What was 'good' for the Thebans was not necessarily what was 'good' for the Athenians. As Antiphon the Sophist put it, 'justice consists in not transgressing any of the ordinances of the state of which one is a citizen' (in Davies, 1978, p.120). The Sophists' position thus entailed that justice was relative to a particular polis and that the laws of a polis could not be criticised as unjust. The critique waged on this by Plato and Aristotle was to claim, in their different ways, that virtue was not determined by convention but by nature (*physis*).

To Plato the Sophists' teaching made justice a matter of opinion and not knowledge. Opinions can differ as to whether something is the case but when something is known to be the case then those who possess this knowledge are at one with each other. It was because the Sophists dealt merely with opinion that they saw the variability and diversity of justice as basic. Whereas, on Plato's understanding, justice as the object of knowledge was unchangeable. The just society for Plato was one that reflected in its organisation the immutable Form of Justice (1955, p.238) or archetype ('a pattern in heaven' (p.369)) that could be rationally known and in terms of which all communities could be judged. The Platonically just society was one where its members do their tasks – produce, defend, rule – according to their 'natures'. All humans possess three faculties – appetite, spirit, reason – but as a fact of nature in different individuals different faculties predominate. Accordingly those whose appetite is dominant should produce, those who are spirited should defend and the rational should rule (p.183). This natural order Plato believes is reproduced in the individual so that the naturally just individual is one in whom the three faculties are properly organised (p.196). Since this is the one true picture of justice in both society and the individual it follows that its truth is a matter of immutable knowledge and not mutable opinion. There cannot, it also follows, be more than one version of justice. Thebes and Athens are just insofar as they approximate the truly just arrangement. The Sophists are in error when they regard justice as conventional and dependent on the diverse particulars of local circumstances.

Aristotle rejected the Sophist case in the opening pages of his

Politics (1946). The polis exists by nature and we saw in Chapter 1 that Aristotle believed that Man too is naturally a being of the polis. Aristotle tackled the Sophist case head on in his discussion of slavery. According to the Sophists slavery as a social institution was a matter of local conventions and had no roots in nature. But to Aristotle there was in nature a distinction between rulers and ruled; indeed this is a 'general law' (p.35). Hence in the individual the soul naturally ruled over the body, in the family the man naturally ruled over the woman, and the parent over the child, and in the household as a whole masters naturally ruled over slaves. In the same way that it is no local convention that males ruled over females so it is no contingent social arrangement that masters ruled over slaves. There were individuals whose very nature made them dependent on others so that they became the property of another (p.13). While some individuals were slaves because of local conventions, there were in addition individuals who were slaves by nature so that the institution of slavery was not in its entirety a matter of local decision. Significantly because some slavery was natural then it was for Aristotle also authoritative. Natural slaves were realising their end (*telos*) as slaves and therefore slavery was justifiable.

While Plato and Aristotle sought to reject the Sophist teaching that social institutions were purely conventional by invoking a (universal) natural order they do not make much of the idea of human nature in that context. It was in the Stoic notion of Natural Law that the universality of human nature first comes effectively into play. The Stoics built on the distinction between *nomos* and *physis* and were indebted to Aristotle's teachings but the reason why universality became 'effective' in their writings was that they were writing in a world where the self-sufficient city-state no longer constituted the model of political life. The horizons opened up by Alexander the Great and the extent of his rule made the polis appear parochial and antiquated, while the turmoil that followed Alexander's death made the polis an unviable political entity. Stoicism (along with Epicureanism) developed as intellectual reactions to this turmoil. Though the thought of the Stoics and the Epicureans differed considerably they shared the aim of concentrating upon the individual. Self-sufficiency was to be the goal of the individual and not, as formerly, of the polis. It was this factor that gave to the universality of human nature its more overtly political significance.

The keystone of Stoic doctrine was that Man should live according to Nature. This injunction was a mixture of physical and moral theory. The active stuff that comprised the cosmos was a rational fiery spirit (*pneuma*). This spirit pervaded everything and in Man this 'divine spark' constituted 'reason'. The 'natural life' was a life in accordance with reason, which itself was said to be a life of virtue 'for thither does nature lead us' (Laertius, 1961, p.25). Humans, however, were prey to the passions (grief, love, hate and so on) and these disturbed the natural/rational/virtuous life. These passions were a sort of pathological affliction and the goal of human life should be to shun them and attain a state of unperturbedness or 'apathy'. Such a 'natural life' of reason and virtue was enjoyed by the sage. Furthermore such sages, because of their natural sagacity, formed a community in that they had more in common with each other, as exemplars of human nature (see Chapter 2), than they had with their fellow citizens. They were 'cosmopolitans' – citizens of the universe, of nature, rather than any particular polis (Baldry, 1965, p.108). Although at first confined to the exceptional sages, later Stoic thought emphasised the universal possession of reason so that all are fellow-citizens for now the 'world is in a manner a state (*polis*)' (Aurelius, 1961, p.124).

To the Stoics, though the rigour with which they subscribed to this doctrine weakened, whatever is not conducive to virtue is a 'thing indifferent'. To value, or in any way to invest with significance, that which is indifferent to virtue is to become perturbed and to lose virtue. The criterion of indifferency is neatly summed up by Seneca, we ought not to regard 'as valuable anything that is capable of being taken away' (1969, p.52). By this criterion not only wealth and status but also health and indeed life itself are to be numbered among indifferent things. We now come to the political significance of this emphasis on universality. The effect of Stoic teaching was to undercut the social dimension to virtue (*arete*) that was characteristic of earlier Greek thought. While Aristotle, as we saw in Chapter 2, thinks rationality is the defining quality of Man he believes that it is only attainable given certain social preconditions. Aristotle had defined the polis as 'an association of free men' (1946, p.113) but he meant, in effect, by this definition that only the heads of households can qualify as free men. This is because all their needs were taken care of *within* their household so that in the polis as such they were not dependent on any other individuals. Conversely, for the Stoics because of the universal physical possession of reason then a rational life was, in principle, in the grasp of all.

It is symptomatic of this universality that the two chief exponents of this later Stoicism were Epictetus (AD 55–135), who was a slave, and Marcus Aurelius (AD 121–180) who was an Emperor. With virtue severed from status a slave could be defined as 'one who can be restrained or compelled or hindered or thrown into any circumstances against his will' (Epictetus, n.d., p.349). This, of course, now permits in principle the turning of the rich into slaves and of slaves into free men. Anyone who values life for its own sake can be convicted of slavery and, as Seneca (a very wealthy individual) makes plain, 'all life is slavery' (1961, p.70).

By linking Man's universal possession of reason with Nature, and by linking that with virtue, this possession had great normative weight. A principal manifestation of this normativity was, as a corollary of membership of the universal city (cosmopolis) of reason, the superiority of the universal law of reason over the particular laws of different cities. While Athenian law might differ from Theban law, both of these, if they were to command the assent and obedience of rational Man, must be in conformity with Nature's own rational prescriptions – Natural Law.

Aristotle had in passing remarked that there was a universal law 'which is conformable merely to the dictates of nature, for there does exist naturally an universal sense of right and wrong, which in a certain degree, all intuitively divine, even should no intercourse with each other, nor any compact have existed' (1910, pp.86–7). This Natural Law, according to Cicero, was 'eternal and unchangeable, binding at all times upon all peoples' (1929, p.216). It was a mistake, Cicero claimed, to assume from the diversity of social customs and laws that justice was purely a matter of local convention. To make such an assumption would be to deny the 'true nature of man'. It would deny that there was in human nature any requisite universality. This universality was needed to enable the Law of Nature to be binding on all.

Whence was this Law derived? Cicero's answer was God or Nature. It can easily be appreciated how this notion of a superior law, emanating from a superior law-giver, was incorporated without difficulty into Christianity. As developed by Aquinas, Natural Law became the bedrock of Christian jurisprudence.

Natural Law for Aquinas was the fruit of Man's reason participating in the order of Divine reason. Humans were distinctive in this regard for 'Man is made in the image of God' (1969, p.1). This gave to human nature a special normative status. There could accordingly be attributed to human nature a universal end or purpose and a set of universal natural inclinations (such as the ability to form true judgments and evaluations) to serve that end.

Among the manifold consequences of the Reformation was a weakening of this direct theistic interpretation of Natural Law. Nevertheless the role of a superior normative order was still needed, indeed even more so due to the violent clashes between Catholic and Protestant and increasing knowledge of peoples to whom the Gospel was unknown. As one development of this, although this is of course to simplify a complex story, new systems of Natural Law were drawn up – notably by Grotius, Suarez and Pufendorf – which attempted to base this law more directly on human nature. As Grotius put it 'the very nature of Man . . . is the mother of the Law of Nature' (1957, p.13). Since the normative force of this Law is now traced to human universality it entails that even infidels are able to know in their hearts and minds the lessons of this Law and thereby maintain a just society. One practical application of this was to deny legitimacy to the spoliation of the New World on the grounds that its inhabitants were heathens (Skinner, 1978, vol. 2, p.169).

We can pause here to note again how the use of the idea of human nature in political discourse – in particular the utility of its facet of universality – came into salience in conjunction with increased awareness of diversity. Whole societies were discovered that differed radically from those familiar to Europeans. As Spinoza put it 'experience has revealed all conceivable sorts of commonwealth, which are consistent with men's living in unity' (nd. p.288). Yet as Spinoza went on to note this diversity also revealed that 'all men, whether barbarous or civilized, everywhere frame customs, and form some kind of civil state' (p.290) and this universality, Spinoza believed, was to be explained by the universal properties of human nature.

In the eighteenth century there developed an increasing emphasis upon the Natural Rights possessed by Man. Thus in the American Declaration of Independence it is held to be 'self-evident' that all men are endowed with 'certain inalienable rights' and that among these rights are (famously) life, liberty and the pursuit of happiness (Becker, 1942). These rights are the corollary of human equality which itself can only be understood normatively; the rights are 'endowed' by Man's creator. Being derived in this manner it means that they are not given by Man and therefore cannot be taken (or given) away by Man; hence they are inalienable (an attribute missing from seventeenth-century rights theory). The political thrust of this theory is apparent from its context. The Americans had just broken away from their political ties to the British state. The justification for this action was that British rule was tyrannical and as such had forfeited the right to expect obedience. The purpose of every government was to secure the inalienable rights of Man and if it fails to do that then 'it is the right of the people . . . to institute new government'.

These inalienable rights pertain to the nature of Man. There is in virtue of this what Paine called the 'unity of Man' (1948, p.53). Human nature as human nature is not confined to any specific time or place. This is the point behind the convention of a State of Nature or 'natural condition of mankind'. It was not thought either morally or politically significant by Hobbes, Pufendorf, Locke and others that existing civil societies seemed to differ widely in political practice or precept. Regardless of its location, government to be effective must be absolute *because* of the operation of Man's 'natural passions'; or government to be legitimate must rest on the consent of the governed *because* of Man's natural equality, freedom and independence.

As a final illustration of the pervasiveness of universalism we can cite the work of Jeremy Bentham. Bentham is chosen, because while he was the major contemporary opponent of natural rights theory, his thought too was universalist and, moreover, his universalism also stemmed from his account of human nature. In addition, Bentham represents a prominent strand in Enlightenment thought. Confronted by the now extensive evidence of the diversity of human life the thinkers of the Enlightenment did not embrace relativism but sought universal constants. They sought common principles to be found in all societies and in terms of which all societies could be judged. Human nature served conspicuously as one of these universals (Berry, 1982, Ch.1).

The very first sentence of Bentham's *Principles of Morals and Legislation* reads 'Nature has placed mankind under the governance of two sovereign masters, pain and pleasure'. Behind Bentham here lies Hobbes, with his universalism based on pleasurable appetites and painful aversions; Hartley, with his associationism whereby the 'vibrations' of the human mind operate universally in such a way that the associations attending pleasure and pain are accelerated and strengthened (1810, vol. 1, p.81); and Hume, to whom the universal patterns of association constitute 'regular springs of human action and behaviour' so that 'mankind are so much the same in all times and places' (1955, p.93). The practical dimension of Bentham's theory of human nature is made explicit in the sentence that immediately follows that just given for there he comments that it is for the two sovereign universals of pain and pleasure alone 'to point out what we ought to do as well as to determine what we shall do'. Furthermore just as the logic, and political point, of Natural Rights was to undercut any social and cultural particularity so too does Bentham's utilitarianism.

For example, in his essay *Of the Influence of Time and Place in Matters of Legislation* Bentham devoted some attention to the application of his doctrine in different societies. Given that the aim of every good law was to prevent mischief and given also that this mischief was reducible to a quantum of pain and given further that human nature was universal, then laws can be reformed and even transplanted from one society to another. It was no obstacle to such reform that there was great diversity between societies. Though there may well be considerable local variations in, for example, property laws yet that variety merely overlaid a universal and effective substratum. In short, 'all places are alike', so that laws may be transplanted from one place to another and these would be accepted because 'really useful changes . . . produce a conviction of their utility' (1859, p.181).

What this cursory overview of a prominent strand in Western theorising reveals is not merely a persistent strain of universalism but also the attribution of normative significance to the universality. The claim is not that humans happen to share certain common features but rather that by virtue of its universal structure (whether this be located in the possession of reason or emotions) human nature is politically significant (whether this be in the generation of a binding set of rights and duties or of maxims of utility). These prescriptions take their force from human nature where such 'nature' is conceived as *natura naturata*, that is, conceived 'in its passive capacity as an established system' (Hampshire, 1962, p.46). What gave it this quality of 'establishment' was precisely its 'passivity' or indifference to the variable conditions of time and space. This indifference served the political function of providing an Archimedean point in terms of which all local – that is temporally and spatially specific – edicts, laws, customs, policies and so on could be judged.

5 The Debate over Universalism

This chapter falls into two parts. The first examines the critique of the universalist tradition that we traced in Chapter 4. The second examines the variety of the responses that were made to this critique. Our treatment, however, is not exclusively historical because the debate which commenced in the late eighteenth century is still very much alive.

The critique of universalism

It is probably fair to say that Bentham's confidence that laws can be transplanted now causes some uneasiness. The reason for this is that 'our' sensibilities and intellectual convictions have been informed by the assault made on universalism that commenced contemporaneously with Bentham.

Politically the assault on universalism is best grasped initially by examining the theory of nationalism, as outlined in the late eighteenth-century and early nineteenth-century. The normative base of nationalism lies in the investing of value or normative significance in the specific and the temporal rather than in the uniform and universal (Berry, 1981). In other words, for a nation to claim that it ought to be self-governing it requires an identity as a 'self'. This identity is attained through differentiating itself from others (specificity) and from appropriating to itself a continuity through time (temporality). The link between this normative nationalism and human nature is to be found, in principle, in the writings of Herder. Herder articulates what I have called the 'contextualist' theory of human nature (Berry, 1982). According to contextualism, human nature is unintelligible outside its specific cultural context. As we have seen, to the universalist (until the eighteenth century at least) the particular societies in which individuals lived was irrelevant because such particularity could not affect their status as sinners or bearers of Natural Rights or their susceptibility to pleasure and pain. Of course, there were differences between societies but, as Bentham's thought exemplifies, these were less significant than this universalist core.

In contrast to this universalism Herder accepted the differences between societies. He did not try to explain them away as the merely contingent aspect of a more significant uniformity. For Herder each different form of cultural experience was of intrinsic value and, as such, was worthy of being valued. As he put it in his critique of Voltaire, Hume and their German counterparts 'each nation has its centre of happiness within itself' and human nature is not the vessel of an 'absolute, unchanging and independent happiness' but is a 'pliant clay which assumes a different shape under different needs and circumstances' (1969, pp.185–6). There is no suprahistorical universal norm of happiness or human nature in terms of which all societies can be placed in some rank order. His crucial point is made explicitly in his travel diary, written in 1767, 'Not a man, not a country, not a people, not the past of a people, not a state are like one another. Consequently, the true, the beautiful and the good in them are also not alike' (1871, p.472).

Each culture should be treated on its own merits. Since there is no universal norm then comparison, and thence even more emphatically judgment, between cultures or societies is meaningless. To Herder human nature was embodied in culture and it could only be understood in terms of this embodiment. Importantly it is in language that Herder finds the key to what makes a culture what it is. The speech of (so-called) primitive Man does not, as was commonly held to be the case, consist of automatic meaningless responses to external stimuli but is the bearer of meaning. This is the case because on Herder's understanding language is indistinguishable from mind or thought (1969, p.132). The language humans speak expresses who they are. Given that language has this intrinsic expressive function then different languages express different cultures. This is the thrust behind the concept of a *Volk*. Those who speak the same language share the same experience. This experience is what makes them what they *are*, gives them their identity, and what thereby distinguishes them radically from others. This point is made emphatically within a nationalistic political framework by Fichte when he declares 'those who speak the same language are joined to each other by a multitude of invisible bonds . . . they understand each other and have the power of continuing to make themselves understood more and more clearly; they belong together and are by nature one and an inseparable whole' (1968, p.190).

The consequence of this contextualism is that human nature can no longer function as a meaningful universal but can only be comprehended within its specific cultural context. The culture is the specific embodiment of a people's way of life, *its* way of making *its* sense of the world. Though primitive rituals and beliefs might appear (to the civilised mind of the *philosophe*) to be meaningless mumbo-jumbo that is no warrant to dismiss them because the 'true, the beautiful and the good' are specific to particular cultural complexes. The particular language spoken not only distinguishes the speakers from those with a different tongue it also furnishes them with a specific understanding of the world (Whorf, 1956, p.252).

This understanding involves an inventory of the world's contents (240 expressions for the colour of horses' hides are available to the Argentinian gaucho (Steiner, 1975, p.87)) and its categories (in Shambala there is only 'today' and 'not-today' and thus no linguistic distinction between yesterday and tomorrow (Cassirer, 1953, vol. 1, p.221)). It also involves the very conception of personhood (there is no single word for the first person pronoun in Japanese, rather the word used depends on the circumstances of its use (Pedersen, 1979, p.85)). The conclusion drawn from regarding linguistic facts of this sort to be salient is that language and culture form an inextricable whole and that culture is not some optional prop that humans possess but is necessary to them for 'it is through cultural patterns, ordered clusters of significant symbols that man makes sense of the events through which he lives' (Geertz, 1972, p.363).

The emphasis placed by Herder on language did therefore open the way to interpretations of human nature that stressed the importance of language and symbolic interaction more generally. For example, to Ernst Cassirer, who paid fulsome tribute to Herder's work, Man is best understood as *animal symbolicum* (1944, p.26). The language, the myths, the art and so on that an individual experiences are not some incidental facet but are constitutive of social identity. Any idea of human nature understood as pertaining to any individual anywhere is necessarily an uninformative empty abstraction, for without this social identity the individual is nothing. As Berger and Luckmann express it 'human-ness is socio-culturally variable' because 'Man's specific humanity and his sociality are inextricably intertwined. Homo sapiens is always and in the same measure homo socius' (1966, p.67, 69).

Aside from providing a conceptual underpinning for nationalism, this contextualist reading of human nature can be used to criticise all individualist understandings of politics, such as Locke's (see Chapter 1). A culture, like a language, is not the product of an individual. Just as language is neither invented nor its usage a matter of individual choice or caprice so the individual is similarly born into an on-going community. An individual's culture is not some separable external means to be exploited at will in order to attain independent goals but is, rather, the context within which the individual conceives of himself or herself as an individual (with attendant goals). This context (language, religion, art, politics, customs) is irreducibly social. The inevitable exposure of the individual to these social forces establishes a basic disposition. This disposition constitutes a second nature which is not perceived as an independent 'object' distinct from the self. In Ruth Benedict's metaphor this disposition is the lens through which one sees rather than what is seen and, accordingly, it is in terms of it that judgment is passed as to what is natural or normal (1968, p.7). As we noted in Chapter 1, it is this process to which Burke was drawing attention with his quite deliberately named notion of a 'prejudice'. A prejudice is

'of ready application in the emergency; it previously engages the mind in a steady course of wisdom and virtue and does not leave the man hesitating in a moment of decision, sceptical, puzzled and unresolved. Prejudice renders a man's virtue his habit; and not a series of unconnected acts. Through just prejudice his duty becomes part of his nature.' (1882, p.359)

These prejudices are constituted by social practices established through time. These practices cohere into traditions. It is through such traditions that individuals participate in a whole greater than themselves. As conservatives have long emphasised (cf. Berry, 1983) individuals only understand themselves, and they in their turn can only be understood, in supra-individualist terms. Symptomatic of this is the distinction between Burke's idea of the social contract and the standard liberal/individualist version of that idea. To Burke this contract serves to establish the corporate identity of the polity, hence it is conceived as a partnership 'between those who are living, those who are dead and those who are to be born' and not as a 'partnership agreement in a trade of pepper and coffee, calico or tobacco or some other such low concern to be taken up for a little temporary interest and to be dissolved by the fancy of the parties' (1882, p.368). Yet it is this latter commercial conception that serves as the model for the liberal idea. The social contract of liberal political theory turned political life into a cost/benefit calculus whereby independent individuals came together to pursue their mutual yet separate interests. This entails that the state is merely a means to the furtherance of the individual's ends (as in Locke's definition that the purpose of government is the protection of property) and, in addition, though this point is much clearer in Hegel's rejection of the social contract than in Burke's, it entails that these ends themselves can be known, valued and formulated prior to the state (Berry, 1977).

To summarise this part: by conceiving human nature as specific to time and place contextualism was (and is) a powerful critique of universalism. Whereas any one individual was in universalist terms interchangeable with another, contextualism drew attention to differences. The political import of this is apparent. Universalism was and is criticised from both the Right and the Left. Joseph de Maistre remarked with respect to the French Constitution of 1795 that it

'was made for man. But there is no such thing as man in the world. During my life, I have seen Frenchmen, Italians, Russians and so on; thanks to Montesquieu, I even know that one can be a Persian; but I must say, as for man, I have never come across him anywhere.' (1965, p.80)

A Constitution, it followed, that was made for all nations was in reality made for none. To use the empty abstraction 'Man' as the basis for political theory is to indulge in idle speculation and to use it as the basis for political practice is (literally) to do violence to the particularity of a society's institutions.

While de Maistre provides a contextualist critique from the Right the critique from the Left similarly berates the abstractness that it attributes to liberal theories of human nature. This abstractness is generally put down to the presence of bourgeois market assumptions. These assumptions, which reflect the historical status of Man now bereft of the social ties that had been characteristic of feudalism, take humans simply as beings who are intent on maximising their own interests. Marx gives classic voice to this in his assessment of Bentham as a 'genius in the way of bourgeois stupidity' who 'takes the modern shopkeeper, especially the English shopkeeper, as the normal man' so that 'whatever is useful to this queer normal man, and to his world, is absolutely useful' (1967, vol. 1, p.608). This asocial abstract universalism – Man as Man – has even been seen by Foucault as the source of the very concept of 'human nature'. 'Man', Foucault claims, is a recent creature, not existing conceptually until the end of the eighteenth century (1970, Chs 9 and 10). Regardless of Foucault's own preoccupations it is the case, as we shall see in Chapter 7, that 'human nature' is viewed with suspicion by the Left because of the conservative ideological uses to which it is put. While socialists and conservatives have a common enemy in liberalism, since they share an anti-individualist perspective, the latter's recourse to human nature to substantiate, for example, the ubiquity of hierarchy and custom is mistrusted by the former because of the backing it thereby gives to the status quo.

The critique of contextualism

If we pause to reflect on this account of contextualism an apparent paradox presents itself. Contextualism developed as a reaction to eighteenth-century universalism – to talk of mankind being the same in all times and places, whether in terms of the possession of rights or of the susceptibility to pleasure and pain. Yet contextualism is clearly itself a theory of human nature; Man's nature is constituted by the specific cultural context within which it is ineluctably to be found. As a theory of human nature contextualism must couch this in universalist terms; *all* humans are contextually constituted. But can there be a meaningful or cogent theory of specific universalism?

To answer this question a number of issues must be confronted. One way of arriving at a negative answer to the above question is to argue that contextualism, if pushed to its logical core, leads to relativism and then to maintain that relativism entails the rejection of universalism so that contextualism lacks cogency.

Relativism

In general terms the move from contextualism to relativism can easily be made. Since a contextually defined human nature is one that is inseparable from its specific cultural setting, and since there are many different cultures, human nature cannot function as a trans-cultural constant. What one culture, in its practices and institutions, assumes to be 'human nature' and therefore universal to mankind may be quite different from what another culture, with different practices and assumptions, assumes to be 'human nature'. It is arguably indicative of this that in many languages the word for 'mankind' or 'human being' and the word for one's own tribe is identical. Given the internal connexion between a theory of the nature of Man and an account of human conduct (examined in Chapter 2), for this account to be used to judge other cultures (with their own standards) is merely an expression of parochiality; each is valid in its own terms, there is no overarching scheme of evaluation. What appears essential in culture *A* may lack that status for culture *B*. There is no neutral point of reference. Accordingly, the fact that culture *B* accepts a custom, which according to culture *A* is contrary to human nature (destroying property for example), can always be accommodated. This accommodation can be made by labelling this custom inessential so that it is judged to be a random pathological manifestation of personal caprice. Alternatively it may be accommodated by being subsumed under a category acceptable to culture *A*, so that the destruction of property is 'really' an example of the maintenance of social status.

In this way the notion of human nature can be seen to be self-validating. To say that a notion is self-validating is to say that it cannot be refuted. If, for example, it is argued that Man is essentially rational then any 'irrational' act put forward as evidence to refute this argument becomes merely inessential and not a truly 'human' act. But this now makes the attribution of rationality uninformative. Man as a rational being acts rationally by dint of definition not evidence. The notion of a universal essence of human nature is thus no better than an empty tautology, akin to the statement that a black cat is a cat.

If this move from contextualism to relativism is recognised then two alternative readings of its import are possible: *either* the conclusion is positively accepted and relativism is embraced so that the universalist pretensions of the concept of human nature are dismissed, *or* the conclusion is judged to be a reductio ad absurdum so that it is the contextualist premises that must be dismissed. The latter alternative is the one which is more commonly accepted. This preference is based on the demonstrable untenability of the relativist case *and* the apparent indispensability of the concept of human nature.

Philosophically, relativism has few defenders. Barry Barnes and David Bloor (1982), who do defend relativism, put this hostility down to non-philosophical factors such as political ideology. The Right, on this view, are opposed to relativism because they see it as destroying the defences against Marxism and totalitarianism, and the Left are opposed because they see it as sapping the commitment needed to overthrow the bourgeois status quo by denying that there is a secure vantage point from which to engage in this overthrow (p.21). Barnes and Bloor, like Mary Douglas (1975, p.xvii), also attribute this hostility to the fact that relativism is perceived by academics as a threat to their moralising (Barnes and Bloor, 1982, p.47n). Ironically this distinction between academics (philosophers) and non-academics is precisely what Barnes and Bloor are arguing *against*.

The lynch-pin of Barnes and Bloor's defence of relativism is a monistic belief that all beliefs are on a par. By this they mean that any one belief cannot be held to be more credible than any other belief (p.25). To argue otherwise they claim is to support dualism. Rationalism is a species of dualism par excellence because it holds that rational beliefs are explicable 'internally' by virtue of the very fact that they are rational whereas irrational beliefs are effects causally explicable by 'external' factors. Barnes and Bloor, in contrast, insist that causal empirical explanation for the credibility of *all* beliefs must be sought. They hold (p.23) that among the relevant questions to ask are, is the belief enjoined by the authorities in the society? Is it bound up with patterns of vested interest? Is it supported by accepted agencies of social control? Barnes and Bloor openly acknowledge that these questions must also apply to their work. This entails their recognition that their own use of words like 'true' and 'false' or 'rational' and 'irrational' is tied to their own contexts; in the 'last analysis' these terms only have 'local credibility' (p.27).

Among the standard theoretical objections to relativism is the argument that relativism is self-refuting. Relativists cannot consistently hold their own position, for to claim that *all* is relative is to adopt an absolute or non-relative perspective. It is meaningless to hold, as the relativist allegedly does, that 'men' are so different in different times and places, that there is no common core, because without this core how would we know enough in the first place to know that others were different! The ability to identify differences presupposes some basic agreement because without that agreement it is impossible to judge whether others do have beliefs or conceptual frameworks different from ours (Davidson, 1984).

Additionally, and less abstractly, it can be objected that the relativists's 'evidence' does not hold up. For example, while it is undeniable that there are a vast number of different languages this universal possession by Man of a language is not as uninformative as the relativists like to claim. Although the relativist cannot in all consistency presume any difference, 'language' is more than 'oral noise'. As Steven Lukes, for example, has argued, to speak any language presupposes a universal underlying structure whereby certain constant features, such as a distinction between truth and falsity, are necessitated (1973, p.238). Without this structure it would not be possible to learn another language nor to know if a translation was good or bad. Moreover these distinctions are required in order to enable any human society to function. Every society requires its members to have a stable set of expectations as to what is done and what it is permissible to do. As the arguments of the ethical naturalists (outlined in Chapter 3) attested there is an intimate connexion between what in fact constitutes human well-being and what can properly count as morality. These arguments imply that we should not be misled by the diversity in the values that are seemingly upheld. Voltaire wittily expresses this point when he observes:

'It is said that there are savages who eat men, and believe they do well. I say those savages have the same idea of right and wrong as ourselves. As we do, they make war from anger and passion: the same crimes are committed everywhere: to eat your enemies is an extra ceremonial. The wrong does not consist in roasting, but in killing them.' (1956, p.502)

This example also reveals that it is this same underlying structure that is presupposed by the studies of history and anthropology. These studies are only possible because we are able to enter into others' points of view and make sense of them. As with the earlier argument, the ethical relativists themselves presuppose the possibility of these studies in order to be able to recognise enough to know that moral codes diverge. Though the interpretation of the status of this underlying structure can differ between, for example, regarding it as established by bio-social facts (Horton, 1979, p.221; Dobzhansky, 1962, p.320) or regarding it as established non-empirically by the requirements of rationality (Hollis, 1979, p.229; Walsh, 1975, pp.282–3), yet both concur in rejecting relativism.

Relativism's own internal incoherence bars it from providing a tenable critical perspective on the concept of human nature. Thus there is no vicious circularity involved in using human nature to criticise criticisms of human nature. In so far as it attempts to say something meaningful – to distinguish language from oral noise for example – relativism itself presupposes the tenability of universalism. This means that the positive attempt to criticise universalism presupposes the tenability of what it is criticising. Moreover, since the concept of human nature is central and indispensable to this universalism, the use of the concept in the criticisms of relativism is in this way absolved from the sin of circularity. In sum, to invoke the notion of Man is to reject the relativist claim that transcultural knowledge is unattainable, and since, on this line of reasoning, relativism is the outcome of contextualism then contextualism too must be rejected as offering a coherent account of human nature.

Contextualism refined

Faced with these and similar anti-relativist arguments the contextualists, who, as we have seen, do uphold a theory of human nature seek to sever the link between their contextualism and relativism. To achieve this severance the typical strategy is to distinguish between a true and a false or superficial universalism.

Thus Burke, in subsuming his entire political theory within a Providentialistic framework, whereby every individual has worth, distinguishes between a genuine moral and a specious arithmetical equality (1882, pp.310, 444). The former, by truly seeing virtue in all conditions, does not 'confound ranks' yet in its practical operation, it has 'mitigated kings into companions and raised private men to be fellows with kings' (p.349). In contrast, the latter erroneously universalises man's uniform abstract nakedness and thus proceeds *a priori* to prescribe the proper form of government without due regard to what really matters, namely, the 'infinite modifications' necessitated by the variations in 'time and place' (p.333). To a similar end, Herder, while he rejects the Enlightenment doctrine that human nature is unchanging and claims that it is adapted to specific circumstances, also maintains that truly these circumstances are equal participants in Humanity, which is the manifestation of God's immanental purpose (1968, p.83). Marx's contextualist insistence that human nature, being a variable dependent on the dominant relations of production, undergoes continuous transformation (n.d., p.124) is placed truly within a universalistic framework of Man's species-being as a free creative producer. This true account is distinguishable from the false Benthamite bourgeois view that equates competitive bourgeois Man with the nature of Man.

However, perhaps the clearest example of this dualism as a deliberate strategy is Hegel's distinction between abstract and concrete universals. Abstract universals, like susceptibility to pleasure and pain, treat the spatio-temporal specificity of human life with indifference. No matter when or where humans are encountered they enjoy pleasure and suffer pain. But this makes all humans the same and cannot explain why, in spite of this uniformity, Man is found in so many diverse settings. In contrast the true universal operates as the ground or foundation, as the conceptual presupposition, of the individual and this universality permeates everything particular (1892, p.309). Shorn of its jargon what this means is that the individual is simultaneously defined by a specific cultural context but that this context itself is an embodiment of Man's definitive universality as a free, rational, self-conscious agent (see Chapter 1). Socrates would not have been Socrates, that is, would not have thought and done the things he did, had he not been a citizen of Athens in the fifth-century BC. Socrates, however, was only able to think and do what he did because he dwelt among human institutions. The polis, with its laws, customs, practices and so on, was a specific human creation. But as a human creation it was equally the product of Man's universality in the shape of free-will and reason. To understand Socrates is, therefore, to understand both the particular (or the concrete) and the universal. This embodied context (the Greek polis) is then placed by Hegel within the progressive development of Spirit through time, which is (contrary to relativism) able to act as a court of judgment from the universalist perspective of world-history (1942, p.216).

What we have in each of these cases is a recognition that there must be established, in Martin Hollis's phrase (1970a, p.214), a 'bridgehead' between the diverse contexts in which Man is necessarily found if the 'slide' from contextualism to relativism is to be avoided. It might still be thought that the contextualist solutions are either self-contradictory (Marx) or evasive through their evocation of Providence (Herder and Burke) or the Absolute (Hegel). In particular, it might seem as if the universality of human nature, as opposed to that of history or God, has been lost.

A notable modern attempt to refine contextualism, while remaining free from the above evasions, is the work of Clifford Geertz (1972). Geertz denies that human nature and culture can be separated (p.35) and he takes issue with the common assumption that the essence of humanity is most clearly revealed in what is uniform rather than in what is distinctive to particular cultures (p.43). To Geertz humans are 'completed' by culture; they are 'cultural artifacts' (p.50–1). In short, becoming human is becoming individual and we become individual under the guidance of cultural patterns, historically created systems of meaning which are 'not general but specific' (p.52). The universality of human nature thus lies in the way that culture channels innate capacities into actual behaviours. More exactly, Geertz's universalism stems from his acceptance that there are universal existential problems that face humans, while his contextualism stems not merely from his view that the solutions to these problems are diverse but also, more significantly, from his judgment that it is 'through the circumstantial understanding of these unique solutions, and in my opinion only in that way, that the nature of the underlying problems to which they are a comparable response can be truly comprehended' (p.363).

Geertz's theoretical pronouncements are put into – or are the fruit of – practice. Bali provides his chief practical arena. He devotes one essay to the ways the Balinese characterise individual human beings. As Geertz presents them the Balinese possess an interacting system of symbolic structures. This system pertains to their definition of persons, their characterisation of time and their ordering of interpersonal behaviour (p.406). According to Geertz the Balinese depict virtually everyone as 'stereotyped contemporaries, abstract and anonymous fellowmen' (p.389); they also have a non-durational, classificatory notion of time (in that calendars do not measure the rate at which time passes but identify kinds of time (p.393)) and hence they have a formalised, highly ceremonised daily life. Although this interdependency between conceptions of person, time and conduct is, Geertz holds, a general phenomenon yet, and this is his key point, this phenomenon cannot be comprehended by any universalist schema which merely serves to turn any particular expression into a mere instance. In other words, it is uninformative to state that Balinese conduct is comparable with conduct Y from culture r, conduct Z from culture s and that all are instances of general rule A.

Geertz's position does have a bearing on politics. Just as the first contextualists were intimately involved in the articulation of nationalism so Geertz uses his refined form of contextualism to explain the appeal to (and of) nationalism in the 'new states' of the Third World (cf. p.320). Since to Geertz human behaviour is 'extremely plastic', cultural patterns provide 'symbolic templates' to organise social and psychological processes (p.216). It is through 'the construction of ideologies, schematic images of social order, that man makes himself for better or worse a political animal' (p.218). Ideologies like nationalism will be generated when a political system begins to free itself from the immediate governance of received tradition. The ideology gives meaning and purpose to the dislocations and conceptual confusions that such a transition brings. Ideologies are thus on Geertz's interpretation to be understood as 'maps of problematic social reality and matrices for the creation of collective conscience' (p.220). This interpretation enables him to claim that nationalism is not a mere by-product but is rather the 'very stuff of social change' in many new states (p.251). In short, it is, because Man is for Geertz a cultural creation who lives within the world of shared symbols that ideologies play such a prominent political role, especially in the Third World.

Universalism reclaimed

Geertz's refinement of contextualism as manifest in his interpretation of the Balinese, has been criticised by, for example, Maurice Bloch (1977) for assuming that ritual contexts establish *the* cognitive systems of peoples. More specifically Geertz's claim that the Balinese have a non-durational notion of time omits, according to Bloch, the many other circumstances, especially practical ones, like agriculture, where the Balinese employ a durational notion. Indeed, this point prompts Bloch to observe that cognitive universals will be found where Man is most directly in contact with Nature.

This observation is indicative of a positive response to the contextualist challenge. This challenge reclaims universalism by reaffirming the essential correctness of that perspective. There are it is claimed consistent bases for making comparisons so that a universalistic framework can be established. One such framework is outlined by W. J. Lonner:

> '*Biologically* we are all of the same species; *socially* the species is governed by generalised functional prerequisites; *ecologically* the species must adapt to a limited range of geographic and environmental conditions (ecosystems). These three bases likely converge in various patterns to form a finite number of culture types. Once this is done the behavior of individuals within the cultures can be compared along a fourth baseline – the *psychological* which would assume an inter-species commonality of processes.' (1980, p.46, Lonner's emphases)

Of these four bases the first will be dealt with extensively in Chapter 7 and the third will not be pursued save in passing also in Chapter 7, but we can at this point say something about the second and the last. To deal first with psychological universals: if universalism is to be reclaimed then one telling way that this can be done is to show that all humans possess constitutive psychological traits. Along these lines a number of psychological universals have been identified. Aside from basic cognitive processes like motivation, perception and problem-solving there are also emotional universals. Boucher (1979, p.175), for example, concludes a survey by citing from studies of facial expressions and language in many different cultures the consistent occurrence of six emotions – anger, disgust, fear, happiness, sadness, surprise.

More closely connected to our concerns are the various schemas that have been drawn up which identify universal needs. 'Needs' are frequently seen as having a close bearing on politics, both in theory and in practice. One writer goes so far as to claim that 'in order to make a general determination of what is socially desirable it is necessary to be able to identify the basic human needs' and that 'the core of any theory of human nature must be a concept of human abilities, needs, wants and purposes' (Jaggar, 1983, pp.17, 20). Even if that claim is not accepted in its entirety (for a sceptical survey see Springborg, 1981, Appendix) the key point is that recourse to the universality of needs offers a potent way of defusing contextualism.

These schemas of needs adopt a common focus. What is true of human nature, must, because universality is one of its facets, be true of all individuals in all cultures and 'needs' represent a set of objective data that conform to this requirement. It is the very objectivity of 'needs' that is frequently used to differentiate them from 'wants'. While it makes little sense to say that individuals can want something without knowing they are so wanting, it is sensible to say that individuals can have needs of which they are unaware. It is because needs can be imputed to *all* individuals regardless of context that they defuse contextualism.

Where the schemas differ (at some cost to their claims about their objectivity) is in their enumeration of these needs. Malinowski, for example, identifies seven 'basic needs' – metabolism, reproduction, bodily comforts, safety, movement, growth, health – and four 'instrumental needs' – economic organisation, educational influence, customary or legal stringency, political authority (1960, pp.111, 115). On this analysis politics is a universal because it serves a universal function (policing, defence, aggression) derived from the universality of human nature (p.115). To take another example Corning identifies four distinct sets of needs: those relating to the ontogeny and development of the individual; those relating to the maintenance and self-fulfilment of mature individuals; those relating to dependants (mates, progeny, close relatives); those relating to the inclusive social order within which we are situated (1977, p.41). In developing his own argument Corning criticises the model of needs that was developed by Abraham Maslow. Maslow (1943) identified a rank order of five needs: physiological, security or safety, love or 'belongingness', self-esteem, self-actualisation. This schema has been influential, it provided, for example, the theoretical structure of Knutson's (1972) examination of political personality. To take a final example, J. C. Davies, who had also originally followed Maslow, has more recently produced, a confessedly non-definitive, amended list of needs (1977, p.160). Davies now regards security as an instrumental rather than a substantive need and thus reduces Maslow's five to four. Davies's aim from this identification of 'basic needs' is to locate basic behavioural tendencies that manifest themselves politically. By 'basic' is meant 'common to all beings' (p.159) so that these tendencies will manifest themselves 'despite the obvious and enormous significance of environmental cultural influences' (1963, p.3). What all these writers seek to do is 'to delineate the most relevant parameters of the human condition' (Corning, p.21). We will explore what such a delineation involves in Chapter 7 when we examine the facet of givenness.

It might be thought a weakness of psychological universals in reclaiming universalism from contextualism that they implicitly downgrade the significance of human sociality. The onset of puberty, for example, is in many societies a culturally defined experience just as much as it is a psychological and physiological individual experience. Such a weakness would appear to be overcome if it could be shown that Man-in-society exhibits universal traits. An influential way in which the presence of social universals is revealed is by identifying what features appear constantly within all societies. Clyde Kluckhohn surveyed the literature of over ninety ethnographic monographs and concluded that

> 'every society's patterns for living must provide approved and sanctioned ways for dealing with such universal circumstances as the existence of two sexes; the helplessness of infants; the need for satisfaction of the elementary biological requirements such as food, warmth and sex; the presence of individuals of different ages and of differing physical and other capacities . . . equally

there are certain necessities in social life for this kind of animal regardless of where that life is carried on or in what culture. Cooperation to obtain subsistence and for other ends requires a certain minimum of reciprocal behavior, of a standard system of communication, and, indeed, of mutually accepted values.' (1953, pp.520–1)

In similar fashion Murdock, in an oft-quoted article, produces a 'partial list' of items that occur in 'every culture known to history and ethnography':

'age-grading, athletic sports, bodily adornment, calendar, cleanliness training, community organisation, cooking, cooperative labor, cosmology, courtship, dancing, decorative art, divination, division of labor, dream interpretation, education, eschatology, ethics, ethnobotany, etiquette, faith healing, family, feasting, fire making, folklore, food taboos, funeral rites, games, gestures, gift giving, government, greetings, hair styles, hospitality, housing, hygiene, incest taboos, inheritance rules, joking, kin-groups, nomenclature, language, law, luck superstitions, magic, marriage, mealtimes, medicine, modesty concerning natural functions, mourning, music, mythology, numerals, obstetrics, penal sanctions, personal names, population policy, postnatal care, pregnancy usages, property rights, propitiation of supernatural beings, puberty customs, religious ritual, residence rules, sexual restrictions, soul concepts, status differentiation, surgery, tool making, visiting, weaning and weather control.' (1945, p.124)

Geertz calls such lists 'vague tautologies and forceless banalities' (p.41). It is indeed easy to find fault (Murdock (1957) himself later had some, albeit minor, methodological qualms). For example, to label 'property rights' as a universal probably tells us far more about the labeller than about transcultural practices.

A more sophisticated anthropological universalism is to be found in the work of Lévi-Strauss. Lévi-Strauss is critical of the functionalism that Malinowski's use of 'needs' supports as well as of Murdock's statistical approach. The error of traditional anthropology was to consider the *terms* (for example, fathers, sons, brothers, uncles, etc.) and not the *relations* between the terms (for example, consanguinity, affinity, descent) (1968, p.46). Instead of 'sterile empiricism' (p.51) Lévi-Strauss proposes a structuralism inspired by work in linguistics. Underneath apparent empirical differences lie basic identities. These identities are, however, the work of the unconscious activity of the mind, as instanced by the fact that when we speak 'we are not conscious of the syntactic and morphological laws of our language' (p.56). This 'activity' consists in 'imposing form on content and if these forms are fundamentally the same for all minds . . . it is necessary and sufficient to grasp the unconscious structure underlying each institution and each custom' (p.21). The anthropologist's goal is thus to 'grasp beyond the conscious and always shifting images which men hold, the complete range of unconscious possibilities' and, crucially and significantly, these 'possibilities' are 'not unlimited' (p.23). There are, therefore, certain universal forms. But, he insists, this applies only to the 'forms' and not to the 'contents' (1966, p.65). Not unexpectedly Geertz detects in Lévi-Strauss the legacy of Enlightenment universal rationalism and judges that his actual work on kinship systems and classifications can degenerate into 'triumphs of self-parody' (pp.356–7).

These attempts at reclaiming universalism are offering statements about human nature. To compile lists, like those of Murdock, is to make the point that such convergence is no contingency but is the product of certain characteristics of Man. To investigate, in the manner of Lévi-Strauss, the variety of customs is to demonstrate the presence of a 'single structural scheme existing and operating in different spatial and temporal contexts' (1968, p.21). If all societies exhibit universals, whether openly or structurally, then it is highly improbable that they are the product of cultural diffusion from some single common source and if, accordingly, they have been developed independently then it is equally improbable that all cultures should just so happen to have hit upon these recurrent features.

The metaphor of 'hit upon', with its implication of 'accidental', reveals the basic untenability of any argument which would claim that these universal features are local random inventions. But there is a further point. What is universal can, by virtue of its universality, be accorded greater significance than any local variation. In an important sense (again *pace* Geertz) the universal is thought to be more basic than the parochial. What makes this an important point is the methodological assumption, on which we shall have more to say in Chapter 7, that the basic is the more explanatory. Hence, in line with this assumption, it is to human nature that we should turn in order to explain the uniformities that all cultures enjoy. It was this belief that motivated Hume's endeavour to establish a 'science of Man' (1888, p.xix) and Malinowski indeed provides a definition of human nature that makes this point explicitly: 'By human nature, therefore, we mean the biological determinism which imposes on every civilisation and on all individuals in it the carrying out of such bodily functions as breathing, sleep, rest, nutrition, excretion and reproduction' (p.75).

As it has developed, the debate between (reclaimed) universalism and (refined) contextualism has become one of degree or scale. The strength of the universalist 'wing' lies in its insistence that the concept of human nature is needed to render the diversity of human social experience intelligible. The strength of the contextualist 'wing' lies in its insistence that the intelligibility of human nature cannot be divorced from its social setting. Even the most stringent contextualist accepts the idea that 'human nature' plays a significant universalist role and even the most emphatic universalist accepts the relevance of conceptualising human nature as always existing in a context. This common ground between universalism and contextualism should not be taken to preclude all dissent. The challenge to them both in the form of pragmatism, which we will discuss in Chapter 9, is that the differing claims made by universalists and contextualists can be accommodated without needing to invoke human nature at all. Since, however, the key issue in the attribution of universality is the extent to which this attribute has bearing on human conduct, the next chapter will examine three contemporary theories that claim political significance for the universality of human nature.

6 Universalist Political Theory

In this chapter I consider briefly three different contemporary attempts to use the universality of human nature for normative political theory. I have chosen the writings of John Finnis, Martin Hollis and John Chapman because they do attempt in their different ways to establish some substantive conclusions. They do not in other words remain content with using the notion of human nature to establish merely a few formal generalities. Such formalism characterises much current political theory and it (together with some of the difficulties it involves) can be illustrated by John Rawls's theory of justice and H. L. A. Hart's notion of natural law.

It is a crucial aspect of Rawls's strategy that in order to determine a conception of justice as fairness he places individuals in an 'original position' behind a 'veil of ignorance' so that their choices as to what will constitute a just society cannot be prejudiced by personal preferences. However, and this is the point of interest to us, these individuals are assumed behind this veil to desire what Rawls calls 'primary goods' which he lists as rights and liberties, powers and opportunities, income and wealth, and self-respect (1972, p.62). These desires are explicitly said by Rawls to be what anyone would want 'given human nature' (p.253). Rawls (like Rousseau) requires simultaneously some view of human desires ('men as they are') in order to attain some purchase on how society ought to be organised ('laws as they might be') *and* requires that this view be uncontentious so that his prescriptions can command general assent. The way to achieve this latter requirement is to make his depiction of human desires as general or as formal as possible.

Yet the particular set of desires that Rawls ascribes universally to human nature has not been exempt from criticism. More precisely

87

his supposedly formal list has been charged with being effectively substantive. That is to say, Rawls is alleged to have built up his theory of justice on a particular reading of the nature of Man which, because of its very particularity, cannot do the work that he asks of it. Thus Barber, for example, remarks that Rawls's inclusion of 'self-respect' in the list of primary goods is a substantive first principle and further observes that 'the religious believer simply would not comprehend, let alone accept the secular-skeptical premises of the original position' (1975, pp.295, 313). Rawls's formalism or attempted universalism founders according to many of his critics because of the 'culture-dependency' (Gray, 1978, p.233) of his notion of rationality and thence of his whole programme.

H. L. A. Hart's (1961, pp.189ff.) delineation of a minimum content of natural law has been criticised on similar grounds. Hart claims to derive the content of this law from 'the salient characteristics of human nature'. He specifies five characteristics – vulnerability, approximate equality, limited altruism, limited resources and limited understanding. Importantly, he regards these explicitly as 'truisms'. As 'elementary truths concerning human beings' they cannot seriously be disputed. Given this acceptance then it can also not be disputed that every legal system must provide sanctions and 'minimum forms of protection for persons, property and promises which are similarly indispensable features of municipal law' (p.195). However, Parekh, for example, takes issue with Hart for simply accepting these characteristics as universal facts of human nature and for not questioning if they are not rather only 'facts' within a particular social context (1972, p.96). More harshly, Skillen accuses Hart of providing an 'idealistic apology for the status quo' and of ruling out of consideration 'the possibility that society might be organised along radically different lines' (1977, p.108).

These charges in general, and the final one in particular, recall our argument in Chapter 2 which pointed out that judgments as to the saliency or otherwise of 'facts' of human nature were inseparable from judgments about human conduct. It was also pointed out there, that any conception of human nature, no matter how ostensibly formal or descriptive, carries with it an understanding of what it is appropriate for humans to do.

While Rawls's and Hart's accounts are criticised for being

covertly substantive we can now turn to our three theorists who adopt a much more overtly substantive account of human nature.

John Finnis

In his *Natural Law and Natural Rights* (1980), John Finnis is impressed by the universality among the diversity of human cultures of certain basic values. He detects the presence of seven such values – life, knowledge, play, aesthetic experience, friendship, practical reasonableness and religion (pp.86–9). These values are good for 'any and every person' (p.155) and as 'goods' they are not 'abstract forms' but aspects of the flourishing of a person (p.195). Concerning these goods Finnis is emphatic that they are *human* goods. He thus dismisses talk of animal rights because such talk equates 'good' with mere sentience. This conception of human good is needed, Finnis claims, to resolve conflicts in rights. This resolution will be in favour of that which fosters, rather than hinders, human flourishing. In this way 'we' are able to say authoritatively, though of course not infallibly, that art 'is better than trash', that culture is better than ignorance and that anarchic sexuality threatens respect for human personality (and so on) (p.220). In particular we are also able to claim that there are absolute human rights. Among such rights Finnis includes the right not to have one's life taken as a means to any further end, the right not to be positively lied to where factual communication is reasonably expected, the right not to be condemned on knowingly false charges, the right not to be deprived of one's procreative capacity and the right to be taken into respectful consideration in assessments of what the common good requires (p.225).

While Finnis disclaims that his argument relies on the 'term "human nature" ' he nevertheless maintains that the pursuit of these universal basic values is made psychologically possible 'by the corresponding inclinations and urges of one's nature' (p.91). Again while he does not claim to deduce the values from these inclinations he holds that the content of the basic values is parallel with the natural inclinations. There is a 'fit' between what 'anyone intelligent would consider constitute[s] human flourishing' and these urges, drives and inclinations (p.380). This order of nature is also explicitly complemented by three other confessedly human orders – of artifacts (languages, institutions), of actions (habits, commitments) and of thoughts (logic, analysis).

In essence Finnis has provided a firm restatement of universalism which is heavily indebted to Aristotle and Aquinas. He dismisses what we have called contextualism by saying that its protagonists, despite all their claims, do not show that the basic forms of human flourishing differ between epochs (p.50). It is clear, however, that Finnis's confidence stems, though only in part, from finding support in authorities on psychology (he cites Maslow (p.98)) anthropology and history (p.81). That such support is indeed forthcoming rests on Finnis's judgment, derived from citing certain selected comparative work, that there is a 'striking unanimity' among cultures. This judgment in its turn permits him to dismiss the 'assumptions' of 'students' that there are no self-evident practical principles recognised universally by human beings (p.83). He is confident, too, as we noted above, that intelligent individuals will agree on the criteria of human flourishing, thus enabling him to dismiss as 'unintelligent' anyone who disagrees. But the use of anthropology is not the chief prop of Finnis's universalism. His major support (it may be hazarded) is the conviction, which he openly shares with Plato, Aristotle and Aquinas, that reflection on the grounds of human flourishing and principles of human reasonableness leads to an affirmation of a transcendent source of being (cf. p.395).

This brief investigation of the bases of Finnis's universalism bears out the argument in Chapter 2 that the understanding of what is 'human' is inseparable from an articulation of an ideal form of human conduct. The weakness of his position would appear to be its 'definitionism'. To query his substantive delineation of human nature is to risk the riposte of being called 'unintelligent'. It is hard to know what in principle could make Finnis reformulate his notion of 'flourishing'. The sceptical reaction that Finnis's universalism can give rise to is in no small measure due to others being less confident than he in distinguishing 'art' and 'trash' or sexual repression from sexual liberation. This scepticism is due, in short, to a lesser confidence in the persuasive power of an ideal of human flourishing. It is symptomatic of this lesser confidence that a Rawlsian formalism is now the norm in political theory. This in turn indicates the comparative neglect (historically speaking) of human nature as an explicit item in political argument.

Martin Hollis

Hollis distinguishes between two models of Man – Plastic Man and Autonomous Man. Plastic Man's behaviour is conceived as the effect of antecedent causes and, as such, it, in all its versions, portrays Man as passive. Autonomous Man, in contrast, is conceived as an active free agent possessing a rational self (1977, Chap. 1). Hollis in a complete reversal of B. F. Skinner (see Chapter 1) wishes to defend the latter conception. An important element in this defence is the invocation of the universality of human nature. This invocation comes in the form of a claim that there is an epistemological unity of mankind (1979, p.225).

Hollis uses this universality to establish his notion of a 'bridgehead' to which we referred in Chapter 5. It is a necessary condition of communication between two individuals that there is an 'overlap in precepts and concepts' (1970, p.219); there must be shared conceptions of truth, coherence and rational independence of beliefs. This is not an empirical matter but an *a priori* assumption. The bridgehead indicates that assumptions about empirical truth and reference are shared and this thus enables the anthropologist (say) to credit the natives (say) with the anthropologist's own notions of logical reasoning (1970b, p.238). The upshot is that 'Western rational thought is not just one species of thought nor rational thought just one species of thought' (1970a, p.218). It is this idea of rationality that constitutes the epistemological unity of mankind. Man universally is rational. Rational action is understood by Hollis to mean that which is most likely to secure the agent's real interests. How do we know which are the 'real interests'? Hollis's answer is that they are those which derive from 'our essential human nature' (1977, p.100).

Though their necessary presence is affirmed, the political implications of this are not spelt out in any great detail by Hollis. However we are able to perform the required explication since these implications are in line with those typically associated with the notion of 'real interests'. Indeed here we can find one of the most potent uses to which the idea of human nature can be put.

Humans are not truly free (autonomous) unless they are self-determining agents. Obstacles to this autonomy should be removed. This is not simply a question of removing external barriers but also of removing internal inhibitions. In the words of

William Connolly 'constraints can operate on one's ability to conceive and formulate wants and projects as well as upon the opportunity to fulfil those projects already formed' (1974, p.148). It is not simply a question of having one's desires thwarted but also, more profoundly and more insidiously, of not desiring certain things in the first place because they are never even considered possible objects of desire. Such is the nub of all analyses of false consciousness. Connolly himself refers to the 'happy slave', the 'contented blue collar worker', the 'apathetic prisoner' and the 'happy hooker' (p.63) but, of course, the classic case is the proletariat. The proletariat have not overthrown capitalism, that is, they have not acted in accordance with their real interests because they have been seduced into accepting a false self-understanding that capitalism serves their interests. The seductive agents might be ruling class hegemony (Gramsci), or one-dimensionality (Marcuse), or the operation of a legitimatory system (Habermas), or ideological state apparatuses (Althusser). The message is the same. Though the model of Man proposed in these writings might not be immediately apparent, it is, in its basic structure, the same as that put forward by Hollis. Hollis himself remarks that 'autonomy requires a choice of roles in which a man can rationally do his duty. If few men take this course it is in part because few societies offer it': only in a 'Good Society' would men realise their real interests (1977, p.106).

Hollis's use of the universality of human nature, and the implications in it, illustrates two points made earlier. Firstly, it illustrates the argument in Chapter 2 that a notion of human nature is a conceptual whole, with descriptive and prescriptive dimensions. Hollis himself makes this point when he observes: 'a claim about our ultimate interests underpins the analysis of what is, no less than of what ought to be' (1977, p.101). Secondly, it illustrates the observation made in Chapter 3 that the normative authority claimed by a version of human nature need not be heeded. Thus the politically potent idea that knowledge of human nature permits us to say that individuals do not necessarily know their own true interests (and that others might know these interests) can be dismissed as, in Isaiah Berlin's words, a 'monstrous impersonation' (1969, p.133). Again this is a factor that helps to explain the neglect into which the notion of human nature has fallen. It is because any substantive reading of human nature can be challenged that theorists opt for the supposed safer ground offered by formalism. As we saw in Chapter 3, doubts about any substantive view of human nature were prominent in the rejection of ethical naturalism and it was these same doubts that prompted, in opposition to naturalism, the formalism of Hare's moral theory. The acceptance of this formalism means regarding 'human nature' as too flimsy a foundation upon which to erect any persuasive or authoritative political programme.

John Chapman

Chapman (1977, p.304) defends a view of Man as 'pluralistic, unfinished and rational' against a cultural view (contextualism in our terms) as epitomised by the work of Clifford Geertz. In particular, Chapman wishes to deny the implication from Geertz that the Western recognition of individuality is accidental; is just 'another cultural template that a people may or may not happen upon' (p.305). Instead Chapman maintains that there is in human nature a 'universal psychological and moral dynamic' (p.307), a drive to individuality, that has been realised in Western societies. This means that societies like that of the Balinese, as interpreted by Geertz, suffer from 'cultural incoherence' and are victims of 'inappropriate, constricting and stultifying beliefs about themselves and the world' (p.305). Chapman links this kind of individuality with a dearth of rational thinking: there is a positive correlation between the emphasis on rational thought and action and the feeling of inner authority and integrity that is characteristic of human individuality (p.303). In contrast to the East, Western civilisation is 'characterised by legality, rationality and individuality' (p.315). Only in the West has the universal 'rational impulse to coherence' been linked to analytical reasoning, which, in its turn, is conducive to both scientific achievement and political/ legal institutions. The significant conclusion is that 'in the West institutional arrangements, philosophical beliefs and human dynamics came increasingly into congruence. In particular, moral and political thinking reflect and support a long-term trend against arbitrariness and injustice that culminates in liberal constitutionalism' (p.317).

This liberalism is truly a culmination because, for Chapman, to attempt to move beyond liberalism in pursuit of an egalitarian ideal goes 'against the grain of human nature, frustrates human ambition and energy. . . . Pushed to an extreme, pursuit of this ideal infringes freedom, without which everyone will be worse off than they otherwise would be' (1980, p.305). More specifically, Brian Barry's conception of altruistic collaboration (see Chapter 1) is held by Chapman to rest on 'an incoherent theory of human nature' (1980, p.261) and similarly, in the light of the Western liberal tradition, C. B. Macpherson's version of a participatory community (again see Chapter 1) is equally deemed by Chapman to be 'inconsistent with human nature as we know it' (1980, p.308).

In essence Chapman has retraced Hegel's route out of contextualism into history and away from relativism. He has done this moreover by focusing directly on an understanding of the dynamics of human nature and not by imbuing history with some such story as the realisation of the Absolute. Perhaps because of this Chapman accepts that there is fundamental contrariety in human nature and accepts too that the universal drives of human nature can take on various forms. But his key point is that these various forms are not all on a par; rather, some are better or more congruent than others. Specifically, Western liberalism is justified and celebrated because it is the form of policy which best harmonises with human nature. Chapman's answer to those who would see liberalism as a distortion of human nature is to cite the historical record. The fact that his opponents could cite this record and argue that socialism is the more accurate message to read from the moral development that Chapman discerns is testament to how 'evidence' underdetermines (for reasons that we addressed in Chapter 2) the conception of human nature held. It is this same underdetermination that we came across in Finnis's and Hollis's attempts to use human nature as a substantive principle. However since all accounts of human nature can be challenged or contended (see Chapter 10), and this includes ostensibly formal accounts like those of Rawls, this contentiousness is not in itself a reason to dismiss them.

7 Human Nature as Given

One consequence of attributing universality to human nature is to say that it is invariant. This lack of variation suggests that human nature is thus a fixed item or a 'given'. This suggestion is supported by the evidence of Kluckhohn who, in the course of his argument for the universality of human nature, refers to 'biological, psychological and socio-situational givens of human life' (1953, p.521). This givenness is the third facet of human nature and is the subject of this chapter.

To explore the meaning and significance of this final facet we need to return to the distinction betwen the natural and the human worlds made in Chapter 2. There we noted that, unlike the natural world, the human world of art, commerce, religion and so on was, in principle, amenable to political action. We noted additionally that the concept of human nature served to establish the ground or nature and scope of that action. Burke and Freud, to repeat the example, both see religion as part of the human world but their attitudes toward it differ. The crux of this difference in attitude lies in their views of human nature. For Burke a religious life is a constitutive part of what it is to be truly human whilst for Freud it is a 'neurotic relic' to be cast off. To link religion with human nature in the manner of Burke is thus to establish it as a fixed item of experience. It is given that Man seeks the consolations and spiritual enrichment of religion. For Freud it is not a given because it does not represent a constitutive element of human nature but a replaceable product of wish fulfilment. For Burke it is pointless to try to cast off religion, for Freud that is not only a conceivable but also a desirable goal of human action.

The message to be learnt from this example is this: to claim that a feature of the human world is as it is because of the nature of Man is to remove that feature from the sphere of politics. It is taken off the political agenda. Human *nature* properly partakes of the givenness

95

of the *natural* world of granite, seasons, combustibility and evaporation. It is by partaking of the natural world that, to repeat, human nature is removed from politics. But, and this is the crucial point, such a claim when it is made specific (as with religiosity in Burke's case) can itself be easily construed as 'political'. This is precisely why the concept of human nature is, as we argued in Chapter 2, practical rather than theoretical and is, hence, a political issue. It is also why human nature plays such a central role in determining the shape and character of differing political doctrines.

A good illustration of this 'message' in operation is provided by Hume (1888, pp.534–9). To Hume it is a fact of human nature that individuals are governed by interest and that they are more prompted to act by immediate perceptions of interest, paramount among which are their concerns for their own (and their nearest and dearest's) well-being, than by more distant interests. However, on Hume's account of it, social order depends on the inflexible observance of justice, which is in our long-term interest. The consequence is that this order is constantly under threat from the natural preference humans have to make exceptions in their own case in the pursuit of an immediate good. According to Hume, this threat is the originating motive for the establishment of government. Human nature just because it is human nature cannot be changed ("'tis impossible to change or correct any thing material in our nature'), therefore all that is amenable to action is the circumstances. The circumstances are changed by the introduction of civil government which makes the observance of justice the immediate interest of 'some particular persons'. Human nature is thus the given; political organisation, the human response. Once a society has attained any size then, because of the nature of Man, government is necessary. What this example further shows is how the depiction of the content of human nature (and for Hume this involves as we noted the paramountcy of self-interest which is moreover coupled with an 'insatiable, perpetual, universal' avidity in acquiring goods and possessions for ourselves and nearest friends), precisely because of its determining effects on the scope of human responses, is itself inextricably a political issue.

Hume in his *Treatise* was self-confessedly attempting to establish the foundations for a science of Man. He was in this attempt reflecting a common concern to accomplish for 'moral subjects' (the human world in our terminology) what Newton had recently accomplished for the natural world. It has seemed to many since the eighteenth century that it is little short of scandalous that knowledge of Man and society appears to lag behind that of the earth beneath and the heavens above. There has been accordingly a predisposition to turn to science for an answer as to the nature of Man.

Given the prestige of science, these answers will have great cultural authority. Thanks to this authority these answers provide what are currently the most persuasive accounts of how human nature functions as a given. The first part of this chapter will use these accounts to illustrate the facet of givenness. The second part will discuss the criticism that the approach to human nature that these accounts exemplify is ideological.

Scientific Man

It is not part of my current brief to provide detailed expositions of various contemporary scientific theories of human nature but it will be helpful first to note three of the assumptions that are made in them and then to look at some of the lessons drawn by these theorists regarding the human world of practice.

While there are several contending scientific accounts of human nature the overwhelmingly shared assumption is neo-Darwinism. B. F. Skinner, whose behaviourist account of human nature is otherwise at odds with the other theorists I shall consider, nevertheless, does not question that Man is the product of evolution (1974, ch. 3). According to neo-Darwinism the observable structure and behaviour of an organism (its phenotype) are, in conjunction with its environment, a product of the 'blue-print' carried in its genes (its genotype). This genotype changes through time (evolves) through a mechanism of selection. Individual organisms vary among themselves in the details of their genetic material. Those organisms whose variances are best adapted to, or 'fit', their environment will be able to reproduce themselves (their genotype) into the next generation, while those organisms not so well adapted will be less successful at reproduction. The consequence of these differences in successful reproduction is that in the population of the organism at large the well-adapted will predominate. This process applies to all organisms and thus includes Man.

The human genotype shares 99 per cent of its history with that of the chimpanzee. The distinctiveness of humankind derives from the fusion of two chromosomes so that the twenty-four pairs in the higher apes became the twenty-three pairs in Man. The seeming narrowness of this difference means that the biological species *homo sapiens* emerged only recently in evolutionary time. Two significant inferences are drawn from this proximity. On the one hand, there are those ethologists like Konrad Lorenz and Irenäus Eibl-Eibesfeldt who see in the behaviour of primates – their aggressivity, hierarchies and territoriality for example – important indicators of human behaviour. On the other hand, there are those scientists who focus on the emergence of the distinctively human and see in this the basis of the universality of human nature (Dubos, 1973, pp.39–43). The period when human nature emerged is generally called by these writers, and by those who popularise their work, (e.g. Farb, 1978; Ardrey, 1977; Colinvaux, 1983) the hunter-gathering stage. Edward Wilson provides an unambiguous declaration of this when he writes, 'Human nature is a hodge-podge of genetic adaptions to an environment largely vanished, the world of the Ice Age hunter-gatherer' (1978, p.196).

Since the Ice Age change has been cultural. Here is the nub issue. Does this change which accounts for all the diversity of human life make such a difference that a genetic understanding of Man is too remote to be of use, or do the cultural developments stem effectively from this genetic inheritance? Wilson opts for the latter. He expresses the relationship metaphorically: 'the genes hold culture on a leash. The leash is very long but inevitably values will be constrained in accordance with their effects on the human gene pool' (p.167). (In a later co-authored work the metaphor of the leash becomes a principle (1981, p.13)). It is this notion of *constraint* as the expression of the givenness of human nature that will become our chief focus of interest.

Wilson is adamant that human nature must be studied as one of the natural sciences and his chief aim is to create 'an internally consistent network of causal explanation between biology and the social sciences' (1981, p.343). This network is provided by (in its later, refined version) human sociobiology. The nub of this doctrine is the theory of gene-culture co-evolution. This theory is an explicit attempt to meet or deflect the obvious objections that were made at great length (and with great heat) to Wilson's earlier formulations.

The essence of these objections was that sociobiologists presume an insufficient 'gap' between genes and culture. Wilson now admits that the latter cannot be simply read out of the former. Rather genes generate organic processes that 'feed on' culture to assemble the mind and channel its operations. More precisely the process is analysed into three stages: genes–epigenesis; epigenesis–individual behaviour; behaviour–culture (1981, p.349). The key pivot is the concept of epigenesis. This is defined as the process of interaction between genes and the environment during the course of individual human development (1981, p.52). The genes express themselves (so to speak) through epigenetic rules. These rules range from the relatively inflexible primary rules, for example that humans perceive four basic colours, to the more flexible secondary rules, for example that mothers are attached to their new-born infants. The effect of these rules is to

'channel the development of individual behaviour according to the prescription of gene ensembles inherited by single organisms. The behaviour of many individuals creates cultural patterns . . . the behaviour of individual members in particular cultural settings determines their survivorship and reproduction, hence their genetic fitness and the rate at which the gene assembles spread or decline within the population.' (1981, p.344)

This consequence means that Wilson is able to reject accounts of culture that see it as independent of biology. Marx's theory of history is dismissed because it has 'no scientific basis' (1978, p.207) and that deficiency is due to the tendency of Marxism to conceive human nature as 'relatively unstructured and largely or wholly the product of external socio-economic forces' (1981, p.355). More generally Wilson is dismissive of anthropologists like Geertz because their work is basically descriptive rather than explanatory (1981, p.57; cf. Lopreato, 1984, pp.30f., pp.81f.). But this judgment stems from Wilson's adherence to the view, mentioned in Chapter 5, that to identify what is more basic is *ipso facto* more explanatory. Wilson's adherence to this view is indicated by his conviction that biology and culture are causally linked, with the latter being the effect of, and thus explained by, the former. This linkage underlies his notion of a leash principle. The innate epigenetic rules are given so that, regardless of what the society intends, it is governed by them:

'economic policy, moral tenets, the practices of child-rearing and virtually every other social activity will continue to be guided by inner feelings whose origins are not examined. Such a society must consult but cannot effectively challenge the oracle residing within the epigenetic rules.' (1981, pp.358–9)

This oracle can however, via 'deep scientific study', be called to account so that its demands can be understood.

Here we can broach the second basic assumption in contemporary scientific accounts of human nature. This is the proposition put forward by Bacon (1853, p.383) (and reiterated by Hobbes (1914, p.21)) that knowledge of causes is power. To know that the application of heat to water causes it to boil gives the power to obtain (or prevent) boiling water in the future. This Baconianism is coupled frequently, though not necessarily, with the third assumption which can be called, if a shade dramatically, apocalpyticism. The salience of this general conviction that the world is in a parlous state can be gauged by C. D. Darlington's first sentence in the Preface to his *Little Universe of Man* (1978), 'I address this book to those, mostly young, who are, as I am, dismayed by the present state and future prospects of mankind and the earth we live on'. In similar vein Skinner's opening sentence of *Beyond Freedom and Dignity* refers to the 'terrifying problems that face us in the world today'; Eibl-Eibesfeldt refers to 'social crisis' (1971, p.244); H. Eysenck to the 'very real dangers that confront us' (1975, p.231); Wilson to the 'dilemmas' facing mankind (1978, ch. 9); David Barash to its being 'absolutely undeniable that much of the world is in terrible shape' (1980, p.169) and most stridently of all Lorenz observes that

'an unprejudiced observer from another planet, looking upon man as he is today, in his hand the atom bomb, the product of his intelligence, in his heart the aggression-drive inherited from his anthropoid ancestors, which this same intelligence cannot control, would not prophesy long life for the species.' (1966, p.40)

The root of this apocalypticism is apparent in that passage. It stems from the coupling of the view that human nature was adapted to Ice Age hunter-gatherer existence with the judgment that the traits formed then are inappropriate in contemporary civilisation.

Racial bigotry is one such trait, but the favourite example is how the lack of inhibiting mechanisms in humans against killing their fellow-humans has been upset by the invention of weapons (Lorenz, 1966, p.207). This argument might seem to give autonomy to culture and thus defeat the 'scientific' cause. Wilson, however, invokes the concept of hypertrophy to cover this. As an elephant's tusks are an outgrowth of teeth so the social responses of hunter-gatherers have 'metamorphosed' into 'elaborate even monstrous forms in more advanced societies'. But, of course, Wilson immediately adds that the directions such hypertrophy can take 'are constrained by the genetically influenced behavioural predispositions' of preliterate humans (1978, p.89).

The Baconianism of these writers forestalls any fatalist resignation in the face of these dire straits. It is interesting to note a similarity here with the move to reclaim universalism from contextualism that we discussed in Chapter 5. This move was given a special impetus at the end of the Second World War. The work of Murdock, Kluckhohn and Linton (see his revealingly entitled edited volume *The Science of Man in the World Crisis* (1945)) to discover cultural universals was clearly prompted by, on the one hand, recent experiences of Nazism and the atom bomb and, on the other hand, by the conviction (as expressed by one of their popularisers) that 'to solve our current problems, generalisations and theories will have to be grounded on the principles which govern all societies, the common denominators of human existence' (Chase, 1950, p.68). In essence the human world is judged to be in a bad way because policy-makers have not heeded the findings of science. A proper and correct understanding of anthropology, or genetics, or operant conditioning, or sociobiology, or ethology would prevent ignorant amateurs from pursuing policies that are doomed to failure. Such counselling Eysenck, for example, openly admits in his opening paragraph of *Inequality of Man* is the book's 'very simple purpose'. The essential solution therefore is to apply science. Their fundamental assumption, as we have seen, is that Man is a fit subject for evolutionary science – this then licenses them to extend to the study of Man the findings and conclusions of their own scientific research regarding pigeons (Skinner), geese (Lorenz), ants (Wilson), plants (Darlington). What applies in these spheres must also apply to Man.

Having identified these three basic assumptions, we can now

answer the question: what does this scientific knowledge of the nature of Man lead our writers to prescribe? According to Wilson there will be fashioned a 'biology of ethics which will make possible the selection of a more deeply understood and enduring code of moral values' (1978, p.196; cf. Waddington, 1960, p.81; Corning, 1970–71). What will these values enjoin? Given that geniuses are exceptions, liable to emerge anywhere in the gene pool, then this pool should be preserved in its entirety. But this is only a contingency, for with greater knowledge, and with the power which that knowledge will supply, we will have the option of a 'democratically controlled eugenics' (1978, p.198). Our values will be chosen on an objective basis. Like Freud, Wilson thinks that the scientific ethic is superior to religion and will take over from it. But as matters now stand 'human nature bends us to the imperatives of selfishness and tribalism'. It is here that Wilson uses the phrase to which we drew attention in Chapter 2: namely, that anarchism is 'biologically impossible' (1978, pp.197, 208).

We will return to the import of that last comment, but it will be instructive for illustrative purposes to give two other examples of prescriptions derived from a scientific knowledge of human nature. Eibl-Eibesfeldt talks of 'us' taking our bearings for ethical norms 'from our own phylogenetic adaptions'. Derived in this way our norms can enjoy 'a degree of certainty' (1971, p.245). One fruit of this certainty is a proper appreciation of the family. Man, Eibl-Eibesfeldt declares, 'has a sense of family' (1979, p.230). It is in the family that love and trust, the twin bases of human community, have evolved (1971, p.242). Because of this link with Nature, the family takes on the character of a given. This enables Eibl-Eibesfeldt to explain the failure of the attempt made by the Chinese and Russian revolutions, and more recently by Western communes, to abolish the family (1971, p.238). Similarly recent permissive educational reforms aimed at cultivating aggression-free, happy human beings are inappropriate since, if a child does not experience a particularised social bond, then personality disorders are produced. To support this last point Eibl-Eibesfeldt cites Bowlby (1971, p.217) who for his part drew heavily on research into the behaviour of rhesus monkeys and who also, in his early writings, cited the work of Lorenz (1953, p.15).

The third example is provided by the work of C. D. Darlington. To Darlington it is the genetic system that provides the key to the understanding of Man's past and the making of his future. Since the key lies in the genes, sexual differences play a large part in Darlington's analyses. The male and female think differently and behave differently (1978, p.98); indeed they differ like two distinct species and as with 'the differences between the cat and the dog, the environment as a rule plays no part in it' (p.66). Hence it is that,

'throughout the world boys prefer one kind of game, girls another. These differences are sexually and therefore genetically conditioned. They are the beginnings of the distinctions of culture between the adult sexes which dominate the evolution of many societies. How does it happen? The genetic difference between men and women is, of course, primarily prescribed by the needs of reproduction. But in turn it prescribes their differences in occupation and interests . . . in spite of overlap in their range of variation the two sexes are genetically adapted to benefit from these differences which in turn create a divergence of culture between what mothers pass on to daughters and fathers to sons.' (p.130)

What does Darlington feel able to prescribe with the weight of scientific fact to support him? Like Eibl-Eibesfeldt the family is endorsed, it is 'the indispensable basis of human society' (p.259). However, the Welfare State has undermined it by developing impersonal mechanisms and its functions must therefore be returned to the Friendly Societies and the like, where direct personal contact can be retained. Since breeding-systems are the key to human society, then the solution to society's problems lies in controlling propagation. Thus Darlington counsels the provision of free abortion and sterilisation, the countenancing of homosexuality, and the introduction of a system of applied eugenics – whereby males convicted of sexual assault should be offered the option of castration and conjugal prison visits should not be allowed because suspect genes should not be transmitted (p.243). (Darlington is impressed by the higher than random incidence of an extra Y chromosome among Scottish prisoners (p.99) and he holds that the Mafia is a genetically distinct criminal class (1969, pp.610–1)).

There have, of course, been many criticisms levied at this sort of scientific analysis, but it is its broader political repercussions rather

than the possibly idiosyncratic quirks of particular writers that are
of concern. Before proceeding to investigate the ideological
dimension in these repercussions we need to identify more precisely
the general function that human nature plays in these scientific
writings.

This function can be simply stated. Human nature functions as a
given, as a constraint, as a limit. This is a standard understanding of
the meaning of 'nature'. The nature of x is what makes it x and not y:
simultaneously it is its nature that prevents it being y. It is literally a
matter of definition; to define is to establish a limit or demarcate a
boundary. To define in this way is also to identify. Humans as
humans have a limited range of options open to them.

The presence of this limited range means that there is a constancy
and predictability about what humans will do in specific situations.
Indeed this is the context within which the term 'human nature'
frequently occurs in everyday speech. Examples of this could be
multiplied almost endlessly. I shall give just two both manifesting an
unreflective use of the term. A car assembly worker remarked
rhetorically *à propos* productivity schemes that 'if you had the
choice of sitting down and being paid at the end of the week, or
working and being paid the same amount, which would you do? It's
only human nature' (reported in the *Guardian* (London) 13
November 1979). Commenting on the poor performance of a soccer
team a sport's journalist remarked, 'human nature being what it is,
no doubt there are those who have derived enormous enjoyment
from City's plunge down the First Division' (in the *Sunday
Telegraph* (London) 13 January 1980). But aside from these usages
there is a more general point about this predictability. If there was
not this constancy then the action of complete strangers from
different cultural backgrounds would be entirely unintelligible. As
we saw in Chapter 5 that this is not the case is one of the ways in
which the universality of human nature can be used to undercut
relativism.

According to scientific accounts human nature functions as a
given with respect to culture. As Wilson's leash metaphor brings
out, what is taken as a given establishes the limits of action. To put it
more technically we can say that what is taken as a given maps out a
conceptual space. For example, what is regarded as given regarding
chimpanzees, dictates, in principle, whether it is worth devoting
resources to teach them to communicate through sign language. On

the one hand chimpanzees because of their genetic proximity to humans are conceivably able to communicate symbolically or, on the other, because their brain is underdeveloped when compared to the human it is inconceivable they will be able to communicate with humans. The former argument opens up a conceptual space foreclosed by the latter. Since there is, as the large literature testifies, considerable room for disagreement over the conceptual space within which chimpanzees operate then we can expect, given the concept's 'practical facet', that the disputability will be increased many times when the issue is human nature. From this perspective, Wilson and the others can be understood as mapping out the conceptual space within which humans can operate. But this space is the political or human world. So Wilson's declaration that anarchism is impossible means that anarchism has been placed conceptually 'beyond the pale' by the givens of human nature. Similar reasoning underlies Eysenck's stark comment that 'biology sets an absolute barrier to egalitarianism in life as in sport' (1975, p.193).

Ideology

The argument to be considered can be stated – even if a shade long-windedly – as follows: the notion of human nature, with its assertion of the givenness of Man, which serves to demarcate the boundary between the supposedly remediable human world and the supposedly irremediable natural world, is essentially an ideological notion. Though this assertion is not confined to 'science', the cultural authority possessed by that discipline means its dicta will have great weight. These dicta will present neutral, impersonal or objective findings about the nature of reality which hold good irrespective of what humans believe.

Writing on the meaning and nature of ideology is profuse and diverse. Here I want to utilise one basic sense of the term without in any way claiming that this is the only legitimate use. As I here use it the term 'ideology' possesses pejorative associations so that to label an argument 'ideological' is to appraise it negatively. This means that an argument is labelled 'ideological' from the point of view of a critic and *not* from the perspective of the propounder of the argument. To be more specific, a critic will identify as ideological any argument that presents as an impartial statement of the truth what is really the expression of a partial interest. Typically such an identification would be prompted by a particular use of the idea of 'necessity'. If a state of affairs is said to be necessary then it follows that this state of affairs is beyond control and moral censure. It further follows that the promotion of any partial or sectional interests by a necessary state of affairs is incidental and not deliberate. As a result of this being a pejorative characterisation we find that the criticisms of such ideological argument typically use terms like 'unmasking' or 'revealing' or 'disclosing' or 'demystifying' to indicate that the partial interest is being 'uncovered' from 'beneath' the 'veil' or 'appearance' of an ineluctable and thus indiscriminate necessity. Carol Gould (1973), who employs a characterisation of ideology similar to mine (p.21), provides a good example of this language in operation when she observes,

'the social and historical exploitation of women is hidden under the guise of its being her natural biological inheritance to bear and raise children, to be a housewife. This mystification seeks to keep woman in her place by making it her lot; it seeks to make her role acceptable by making it inevitable. . . . Demystification, therefore, means a return . . . to a changed social reality, in which the very basis for these mystifications is eliminated.' (pp.37–8)

To claim of a policy or human activity that it is contrary to human nature is (in that characteristic mixture of description and prescription) to say that it is unworkable. To repeat the crucial point, a statement about human nature implicitly distinguishes between the given natural world and the practical human world. The former, which is the province of the 'natural scientist', sets limits to what it is possible to do in the latter. The appeal to human nature thus serves as a limiting or closing notion. It restricts the scope of effective action by designating these limits as unalterable objective givens. This restriction is not optional but represents the imperatives issued by Science.

The political significance of these imperatives is that the appeal to human nature amounts in effect to counselling acceptance of the status quo. This counselling would run on the following lines. Not to accept the status quo is to defy the authority of Science, which has provided us with a cure for cholera as well as knowledge of atomic particles. This status quo embodies certain universal truths about which it is pointless to complain, let alone attempt to change. Just as 'you can't make water flow uphill' so 'you can't change human nature'. That a status quo favours some more than others cannot be regarded as a conspiracy to keep some sections of the community in their relatively inferior position. Any such differentiation, as between males and females for example, is in tune with reality. The facts of human nature have to be accepted. Thus it follows that political programmes to implement an egalitarian society, to abolish the family, to dispense with hierarchy and so on will founder on the rocks that are human nature.

It is because of these political implications that the notion of human nature as a given can be judged to be ideological. This judgment need focus only on the *effects* of an argument and not on its *motivation*. There is no necessity in unmasking ideological argument to require that its proponents are hypocrites; indeed rather the reverse. The proponents may sincerely believe that they are enunciating objective, 'scientific', truths; they are simply 'telling how it is'. What this appeal to the 'facts' of human nature reveals, as we have seen, is a generally unquestioned assumption that 'science' provides the right answers. Since it has been 'proved' right about the causes of cholera, the structure of the atom, the function of the pancreas then it is a fair presumption that it provides the 'way forward'. The presumption is very evident in Wilson and stridently so in an article by P. van der Berghe. Van der Berghe is contemptuously dismissive of most social scientists and he asserts that if they want to be considered true scientists (and not affiliated to the humanities) they must 'return to their biological roots' and 'throw off their self-imposed intellectual blinkers' (1978, p.35). The best of the social sciences is economics. This accolade has been achieved because economists have accepted 'the selfish view of human social behaviour'. Van der Berghe calls this a materialist thesis for which there is 'overwhelming empirical evidence'. Proof of the superior status of economics is that it is the only social science 'good enough to warrant the regular employment of its practitioners by large corporations and governmental decision-makers' (p.40).

Yet by his very choice of 'proof', van der Berghe can easily be unmasked as providing a crass example of ideological argument. He has simply assumed a limited, partial, historically specific

perspective and writ this large as part of a project to determine the
ostensible, unquestionable, nature of reality. The core of this
criticism is that the characteristics of bourgeois Man,
competitiveness, selfishness etc., have been attributed to Nature
and *then* Nature is turned to in order to explain the necessary
features of Man as competitive, selfish, etc. (Sahlins, 1977, p.35). It
is on this basis that many critics of sociobiology in particular have
picked up on its imagery as betraying a specific cultural bias. More
precisely, and as is to be expected, attention is drawn to how the
language and conceptual framework of sociobiology proceeds in
terms of market rationality. For example, Barash's sociobiological
explanation of the parent/child relationship is expressed as 'when
parents invest in their offspring it is *because* such investment increases
the likelihood that they will become grandparents; i.e. evolutionary
success, fitness, is ultimately measured by the production of
genetically related descendants' (1977, p.302; my emphasis). That
there is a similarity between such 'scientific' language and that of
economics is held, in the influential analyses of the 'Frankfurt
School', to be no coincidence but a product of the 'technical'
manipulative interest. This interest seeks to control the world
(knowledge of causes is power) and has the effect of entrenching the
advantage of the dominant bourgeois class.

Another example of this supposed bias is the treatment of sexual
morality. Richard Dawkins concludes, after making due reference
to the impact of culture, that 'human males in general have a
tendency toward promiscuity and females a tendency toward
monogamy' (1978, p.177). This provides, as Barash openly
concedes, an explanation for sexual double-standards (1977,
p.293). This is the case because female promiscuity is deemed by
males more damaging than similar behaviour by men. If a male has
been 'entrapped' with one female then he wants to be sure that his
investment in terms of time, responsibility etc. is to the benefit of *his*
and not another male's genes. A critic can easily unmask this as
ideological. To cite Kate Millett, patriarchy, whereby the particular
interests of males are fostered and protected, is 'passing itself off
as nature', as an unalterable neutral given (1972, p.58).

Of course Barash and the others strenuously deny that in
providing an *explanation* they are also providing an *endorsement*.
Donald Symons, for example, comments: 'that men and women
differ by nature has no necessary implication for normative

questions' (1979, p.65). But to writers like Jürgen Habermas this very distinction between explanation and endorsement itself betrays a particular ideological bent. By regarding scientific explanation as the provision of predicted effects from causes (a technical cognitive interest) it is ruling out of bounds other accounts of science or cognitive interest as unscientific, as illegitimate sources of knowledge (1972, pp.4, 308). Most especially it rules out an account that is prompted by an emancipatory interest which aims at a self-understanding of citizens so that they may take 'practical control of their destiny' (p.332). However this emancipatory interest is labelled by the technical interest as contravening the ethical neutrality or value-freedom of science. Questions of self-understanding or practice, it is held by those who share Symons's view, *because* they are not technical questions of control (manipulation of causes to predict effects) are incapable of scientific resolution. But the implication of placing practical questions outside scientific resolution is that these questions are also placed outside the scope of critical reason. This is because, from the technical point of view, the exercise of reason is confined to the task of efficiently and economically fitting means to ends. If practical questions are not rational and scientific then they must be questions of individual value preference or decision. By juxtaposing 'explanation', which is what science can objectively furnish, with 'endorsement, which is a subjective decision, this entire technical approach is ideological. By making a 'fetish of science' it veils practical problems and 'justifies a particular class's interest in domination and represses another class's partial need for emancipation' (Habermas, 1971, p.111).

What does this argument (and other less sophisticated versions) that scientific accounts of human nature are ideological amount to? It seems to reduce to the view that human nature as portrayed by these accounts is 'especially relevant to Western capitalist societies' (Alpers, 1978, p.202). The only way that statement is rescued from uninformative blandness is by holding that this relevance is not neutral coincidence. Rather given that 'ideological' is a pejorative label the implication has to be that capitalism is in some respects reprehensible. But, for that judgment to have any bearing on sociobiology, acceptance must also be implied of the doctrine that in Marx's phrase, 'the ruling ideas of each age have ever been the ideas of its ruling class'. The function of these ruling ideas, of which sociobiology must be held to be a component, is to legitimate the ruling class. This legitimation can now be identified as an ideological exercise. The need for (and thence particular class interests of) the rulers is portrayed as necessary, and contrary ideas like egalitarianism are declared to be unnatural, that is, impossible. In this way the naturalness of human nature becomes 'an instrument for domination which elicits deference and resignation' (Young, 1973a, p.403). Work has indeed been done (e.g. Beckwith, 1981) on how sociobiology has been taken up and endorsed at a popular level and almost every critic of sociobiology feels obliged to point this out. The assumption here seems to be that this popular endorsement is evidence of the ruling class's 'hegemony'. It is a means of ensuring that its ideas 'rule'.

These various arguments that the scientific accounts of human nature are ideological carry with them considerable conceptual 'baggage'. This baggage provides several hostages to fortune. Indeed, the entire question of the relationship between 'material life' and the 'world of ideas' is opened up. Fortunately this is not an issue that we need pursue. The important issue for us is that these critics of the ideological use of the idea of human nature have not in their criticisms jettisoned the idea. The next chapter will examine how they attempt to deal positively with the facet of givenness.

8   The Capacities of Human Nature

The conceptual connexion between human nature as a given and the imposition of limits on human action that we examined in Chapter 7 establishes the context for the discussion in this chapter. In particular this connexion must be confronted by those who see this limiting, constraining role as ideological, as illicitly and unwarrantedly foreclosing viable political options, *and* who do not wish to jettison the idea of human nature altogether.

One way of confronting this dilemma is to reconceptualise human nature in such a way that it does not have this constraining function. There are in this reconceptualisation two closely related ideas. The first of these is that humans make their own limits and the second is that this ability to achieve self-transcendence means that human nature is better conceptualised in terms of capacities or potentials than it is in terms of fixed essences. This reconceptualisation will offer 'a liberatory view of the "nature of human nature" ' (Rose *et al.*, 1984, p.x).

Instead of talk of limits to human nature, which only mystifies the processes whereby humans have made themselves what they are (and what they will be), we must, as Robert Young puts it, 'recover our right to define our own nature through our struggles to overcome our limitations. One component of this is the need to demystify the limits of human nature' (1973b, p.263). Young's language here is perhaps misleadingly voluntaristic. Steven Rose is less ambiguous. He has declared, *à propos* of claiming that Wilson has failed to distance himself from the 'particularist assumptions of the dominant racist, sexist and class bound ideology of late twentieth-century Western society', that we must present a 'real science and vision of humanity – one which says that it is the biological and social nature of humanity to transform itself, reach

beyond itself constantly' (1980, p.170). The consequence of having
that vision is to see that what seems fixed or constant is only so
within the historical moment which is always in flux.

Where does that vision leave human nature? Rose does not
develop his argument but the chief consideration, which he perhaps
hints at in one place when he refers to an 'integrated dialectical
account of human nature' (p.169; cf. Young, 1973a, p.430) (though
the phrase is something of a talisman), is to attack the separation of
'nature' and 'the cultural'. Here the former term serves to signify
the immutable given and the latter the work of human agency. This
attack will serve to demystify nature. Nature, as evolutionary
theory itself teaches, undergoes 'shifts' but, more directly, natural
processes are themselves, of course, open to human amendment or
control. As by use of pumps water can flow uphill so by use of
human intelligence human nature can change itself. A frequently
given example of how nature is controlled is the remedy for the
disease phenylketonuria. This disease, which induces imbecility in
childhood, is caused by a faulty gene which in one out of 30 000
cases is inherited from both parents. However, this fault is
detectable by a routine test and a diet can be prescribed which will
circumvent the genetic defect until such time as its potential to cause
damage has passed (after about six years). This, of course, is
straightforward Baconianism and the real thrust of Rose's
undeveloped position must, if it is to be of interest, lie deeper.

The developed argument would go something like this. The
biological and the cultural are intertwined so that neither must be
reduced to the other. This principle is stated (though only in
passing) by Yankelovich: 'Nature does not exist apart from culture.
Each is constitutive of the other. It is misleading even to conceive of
human nature as something that can exist outside culture' (1973,
p.424). Instances of what is involved here are the distinction,
prominent in feminist literature, between sex (biology) and gender
(culture) and the whole debate over IQ. It is a central plank in
criticisms of the latter concept that 'intelligence' cannot be isolated
(and thence quantified) from its necessary socio-cultural matrix. In
both this and the feminist case it would not be necessary to deny that
there is a genetic component. Thus it can be accepted that there is a
genetically caused difference between male and female physiology
and that there is such a thing as congenital idiocy. There is no need
to adopt a blank-sheet approach to human nature that would

disclaim *any* biological input. However, from these biological factors no social implications can be meaningfully drawn because both sexual relationships and intelligence are social categories which are equally definitive of the 'nature' of individuals (Malson, 1972, p.12). It is a mistake, to repeat, to think of 'natural' as categorically distinct from 'social'. Moreover, and significantly, since humans are social and societies change then humans are also variable and changing. Hence when, for example, Victorians referred to the fragility, weakness and so on of woman's nature – whence her unfitness for the suffrage or higher education – they were subsuming the social by the natural. Furthermore these references had the authoritative backing of Science; it was, pronounced one physician in 1886 when addressing the British Medical Association, a physiological fact that women who studied left themselves 'quite inadequate for maternity' (in Sayers, 1982, p.18).

The view that the social and natural are indistinguishable would suggest a contextualist understanding of human nature. As we noted in Chapter 5, contextualism can slide into cultural relativism. Rose's conclusion is redolent of that latter position (with all its problems) when he writes, 'the human nature of feudal preindustrial society was not the human nature of the industrial revolution, is not the human nature of today's advanced capitalism – will not be the human nature of the transformed societies of tomorrow' (p.170). However, if Rose is serious about his desire not 'to debiologise' our understanding of human nature he cannot mean this literally. What Rose's vocabulary and periodisation do indicate is that he is invoking Marxist theory.

Marx can be interpreted as holding a view of human nature that is at one and the same time critical of all historically static notions and yet not given over to relativism because he still affirms there is 'human nature in general' (1967, vol. 1, p.609n). While, for Marx, Man is indeed, as the Sixth Thesis on Feuerbach puts it, 'the ensemble of social relations', these relations are provided with a necessary structure due to Man's productive species activity. Despite much helpful commentary, Marx's own views are still not free from obscurity but what he seems to require is a view of human nature as possessing capacities. Certainly much of his early writing employs that vocabulary. For example he says at one point that Man is 'equipped with natural powers, with vital powers, he is an active natural being; these powers exist in him as dispositions and capacities or drives' (1975, p.389).

The point of having recourse to capacities or potential when discussing human nature is to undercut theories that conceive of human nature in terms of immutable givens – like the genetic basis of behaviour – and yet avoid relativism. What talk of capacity permits is a view of Man as a universal structure which is capable of self-development, of overcoming hitherto existing limits. Humans discover more about themselves in interaction with their fellows. Thus, for example, that 'true' communism has never yet been realised does not justify the conclusion that this is because communism is contrary to human nature. Though he stops short of declaring Marx's vision of 'selfless communism' impossible Barash, nevertheless, claims that 'evolution *is*' so that it is an ineluctable fact that 'at the heart of human behaviour there lies a germ of genetic selfishness' which means that Marxists 'will have a great deal of work to do if they really expect to create their version of an ideal society' (1980, pp.210, 236: Barash's emphasis). To this it would be rejoined that it is rather the case that the circumstances (of alienation in the Marxist canon) have inhibited the establishment of communism and it is these circumstances to which the prevalent conceptions of human nature, as exemplified by that put forward by Barash, are accommodated. Humans, that is to say, *will* exhibit selfishness in a society geared to the competitiveness of the market place. But these circumstances are changeable and 'human nature' is no barrier to this since all its apparent solidity and givenness stems from its fit to a particular, historically generated, set of conditions. The implication here, then, is that human nature is determined rather than it being a determinant. It is thus perfectly acceptable to consider human nature as how it may yet be and not feel constrained to remain within the confines of how it has been.

Typically, of course, this approach has been concerned to establish the inadequacy of the 'has been'. Utopian speculation and 'critical' theory (Apel, 1979, p.135) can both be interpreted as manifesting this approach. One way this inadequacy is revealed is via the presentation of a view of human nature as it can and should be. This view of how human nature 'may yet be' is then juxtaposed to how it 'has been' with the aim of showing up the latter's shortcomings and also, at the same time, with the aim of providing reasons to change it. This would seem to be the rationale behind

Fourier's elaborate investigations into the structure of human nature which we can briefly outline for illustrative purposes.

Fourier, like many others, sought to emulate Newton's achievement. Just as Newton had uncovered the law of material attraction so Fourier claimed to have discovered the law of mental attraction. There is a regular pattern or rhythm in all life and the key to a proper human life is to construct society in harmony with this rhythm. Alas contemporary bourgeois civilisation distorts and represses this rhythm: creating misery, dissatisfaction and frustration in its wake. To demonstrate this Fourier needs a model of unfrustrated life. This model is provided by a minute dissection of the full range of the capacities open to human nature.

To Fourier human nature consists of twelve passions or faculties. There are the five sensuous passions – hearing, seeing and so on; then there are four social passions – Man has a capacity for friendship, love, family and ambition, and then, to keep these in balance, there are three distributive passions – for diversity or alternation, for intrigue and for association. Society should be organised to permit these twelve to flourish. Like most 'utopians' Fourier goes into detail as to nature of this society, which he calls a phalanstery, wherein we can see the 'spirit of God, since it is composed of the twelve passions harmonised' (1971, p.139). The phalanstery will have an optimum size of around 2000 citizens within which all human diversity can express itself without repression and distortion. We can illustrate this by the alternating passion. This passion is defined as 'the desire felt by the soul of periodical variety, of change of scene and occupations, of contrasted situations, of incidents and novelties calculated to excite charm and to stimulate at the same time the senses and the soul' (p.181). In accordance with this passion there will be within the phalanstery not only a varied sex-life but also two-hour work sessions enabling everyone to take on seven or eight attractive pursuits daily. In short, we are unable to understand human nature properly under existing conditions. This understanding will only be achieved when 'we have seen man exercising without constraint the social and industrial faculties of which he is susceptible' (p.119).

What Fourier's explorations bring to the surface is the inherent difficulty of the language of faculty or capacity. How is something known to be a capacity if it has never been evidenced? A potential that has never been actualised is a mystical item: we only know that an acorn is an acorn and not a chestnut because there are oak trees. Graeme Duncan, who confesses a preference for a conception of human nature in terms of capacities, is, nevertheless, careful to add that this capacity does not 'float free' but is always conditioned by circumstances. He admits that identification of the relevant circumstances is contentious and, indeed, an ingredient in this contentiousness is the very conceptions of human nature held! (1983, pp.6–7). Similarly John Macquarrie, who holds that the study of human nature is a study of 'possibility as much as actuality', concedes that there are (perhaps) guidelines within human nature itself which 'the emerging humanity must follow if it is to realise its possibilities' (1982, pp.3–4).

These points can be fruitfully explored via a discussion of the interesting variant of this position which is provided by Peter Winch (1971). Winch indeed seems to want to reconceptualise 'human nature' entirely into terms of 'human capacity'. Winch's argument is more than usually elliptical and he confesses that he is putting the matter 'overcrudely' when he observes 'what we can ascribe to human nature does not determine what we can and we cannot make sense of; rather, what we can and what we cannot make sense of determines what we can ascribe to human nature' (p.10).

The immediate corollary that Winch draws from this observation is that the concept of human nature 'is not the concept of something fixed and given'. If 'human nature' does not determine what is 'sensible' or intelligible then what does? Winch's answer (p.12) is that there is no general criterion. What there is are traditions of thought and activity. These traditions determine the 'space' within which what can be identified as human capacities exist. Winch provides an example. To ask of a given individual 'has he the capacity to understand higher mathematics?', is only a possible question in the context of the problems of higher mathematics. We can, in other words, only refer to human capacity in the presence of certain traditions and it is these traditions which determine the feasibility of asking particular questions concerning the exercise, or not, of the capacity. This is an open-ended process. Discussion as to whether something is humanly possible or not will always throw up new difficulties and new ways of meeting these difficulties. Accordingly, whether or not something is humanly possible, as a function of human nature, is itself a function of discussion and cannot therefore legitimately foreclose what is intelligible.

Much hinges in this argument on Winch's notion of 'discussion'. What is needed for there to be genuine discussion is seemingly some point of contact. Winch admits (p.12) that in the absence of traditions certain questions cannot be asked and, therefore, presumably no discussion can ensue. If no discussion ensues then mutual incomprehensibility seems the consequence. Given Winch's view that it is what we can make sense of which determines what we can ascribe to human nature then, faced with this incomprehensibility, are we not faced with the possibility that those unintelligible to us are thus not human? (cf. Trigg, 1982, p.168). The apparent possibility of discussion rules out the circumstance that these others are brutes, so that the crucial issue is relativism, or the problem of understanding alien cultures.

Winch, however, is no relativist. He is perhaps best known for his observations on the difficulties of 'understanding a primitive society'. Indeed, in his essay of that title (1970), he does invoke certain fundamental, explicitly 'limiting', notions. These – birth, death, sex – are 'inescapably involved in the life of all known human societies'; they are universals (p.107). Moreover, these notions give us a 'clue' as to where to look if we are puzzled about the point of alien institutions. They are clues presumably because they are a point of contact between 'us' and 'them'. If this is so then the reasonable presumption is that these notions do permit discussion to ensue. The upshot of this is that, for example, the knowledge of (discussion about) the practice of Suttee, where widows join their deceased husbands on the funeral pyre, can extend our (that is, Western Christian) conception of what is humanly possible. But this same example also serves to bear out how it is a 'fact' of human nature that humans do not regard the death of those close to them with indifference and it is this which performs the role of a 'limiting notion' and which, accordingly, makes Suttee intelligible. Similarly the reading of Fourier can sensitise a reader to possible forms of human practices and inhibitions. But these possibilities will remain ever circumscribed by the knowledge that sex does matter to humans.

This discussion of Winch reinforces the conclusion we drew from our examination of Fourier. The language of 'capacity' will only avoid vacuousness if it incorporates, as Winch seemingly had to, some notion of 'limits'. This incorporation is perhaps best expressed in the Aristotelian idiom where capacities have to have an end or

telos which determines their 'nature'. In view of this it may now be
legitimately questioned as to what crucial difference there is
between what we may call an 'essentialist' and a 'potentialist' view
of human nature. The logic of the concept of a potential is that (like
the proverbial acorn and oak tree) it is there in the beginning: a
chestnut has not the potential to become an oak. We thus seem to be
back to the question of limits.

Human nature cannot be potentially just anything. Marx's vision
of communist Man in communist society would make no sense
otherwise. This is to say despite Marx's legitimate wariness about
making detailed predictions as to the nature of future society he is
convinced that this society will be communist. His reason for this
confidence is that such a society is in accord with the expression of
true human potential. The same applies to theorists like Owen,
Godwin and other associationists. These writers appear to empty
human nature of all content and to regard it as malleable without
limit. Owen, for example, writes that children who are 'without
exception passive and wonderfully contrived compounds' may be
'formed collectively to have any human character' (1970, p.110).
Godwin likewise holds, as we observed in Chapter 1, that children
are 'a ductile and yielding substance' regarding whom we have,
accordingly, the power to 'mould into conformity with our wishes'
(1976, p.112). But both presuppose a capacity in humans to heed
what is rational when it is pointed out to them. It is only by virtue of
this presupposition, and its corollary that what is rational has by
definition the assent of all right-thinking individuals, that Godwin is
able to look forward to the end of government and Owen to the
dawn of a New Moral Age. Without this capacity there would be no
'leverage' with which to criticise contemporary society for its
irrationality.

If 'potentialists' use the language of limits we can find the obverse
– 'essentialists' using the language of capacity. Barash, for example,
holds that if nothing else *homo sapiens* 'must possess a genetically
mediated *capacity* for culture, learning, language etc.' (1977,
pp.287, 319: Barash's emphasis). In a similar vein the view that the
biological and the social are intertwined, which as we saw
underpinned much potentialist analysis, does not seriously
differentiate potentialism from essentialism. Thus an essentialist
like Wilson talks of 'coevolution' whereby cultural patterns
(themselves the product of epigenetic rules) ultimately – over a

thousand year span – influence the frequency of the underlying genes themselves (1981, pp.265–6). Nor is Wilson exceptional. For example, W. H. Thorpe has written that 'it is probably more correct to think of much of our structure as a result of culture than it is to think of men anatomically like ourselves slowly developing culture' (1974, p.280) and more technically and recently von Schilcher and Tennant have averred that

'culture imbues the environment; and it is almost futile to ignore it, and to look for a "purely biological" environment, when talking of environments as already understood for the purposes of biological evolution. A priori biological evolution is going to produce culturally adapted individuals when an important part of the environment is cultural; and genotypes placed in such environments will produce phenotypes with important cultural traits.' (1983, p.113)

This convergence between essentialism and potentialism should be expected when it is recalled that the current investigation is directed at the issue of a reconceptualisation of human nature and not at denying that the concept has any validity at all. More significantly this convergence indicates that it is integral to the concept of human nature that it does delimit possibilities. This point has emerged not only here but also implicitly in earlier discussion. We can support that conclusion by utilising an aspect of Renford Bambrough's analysis of human nature.

Bambrough (1975, pp.6–11) identifies three constraints on answers to the question 'what is Man'? There are logical constraints. There is a 'logical space' which, though its precise boundaries and configurations can be chartered and measured differently, places a constraint on what can count as a Man. Anthony Quinton provides a graphic illustration of this logical constraint,

'there seems no sense to the supposition that I might have been or that he might change into an ashtray or a daffodil or a Jumbo jet. Certainly the stuff of which I am composed might be turned into fertiliser or the pièce de resistance of a dinner-party in New Guinea. But then I am not identical with the stuff of which I am

composed, I am just made of it. Individuals, then, do have at least
a minimal essence if the determinancy of reference without which
they cannot be identified is to be secured.' (1975, p.33)

This was the point that we made, though less eloquently, in Chapter 7
when we talked of 'nature' as a definition of boundaries.

The second category of constraints identified by Bambrough he
terms 'causal'. These operate as factual restrictions on the logical
constraints. We do, as a matter of fact, share a common
consciousness with all other humans. We are all constrained
ecologically (recall Lonner's framework from p.8) by for example
(though this is not Bambrough's) a limited temperature range.
These causal constraints relate to our discussion in Chapter 7 above
where we referred to the predictability that human nature can give
and relate more fully to the discussion in Chapter 5 and of Winch
earlier in this chapter where we saw that a theory of human nature
provided a universalist basis so that there is some intelligible
common ground between otherwise unintelligibly diverse
experiences.

Bambrough's final category is moral constraints. Bambrough
here commends Aristotle for seeing clearly that 'man has a nature
and that his nature is the guide to what befits his conduct'. This
point underlay our discussion in Chapter 3 where we saw that a
theory of human nature functioned to make non-contingent, not
arbitrary, the relationship between what humans are and what they
find of value.

Constraints or limits are an inescapable corollary of the concept
of human nature. This point has been made in different contexts in
earlier chapters. We saw in Chapter 3 that a crucial component in
ethical naturalism was the claim that morality is not free-floating
but is tied to human interests and purposes which thus limit what
can be properly said to be a matter of morality. We saw in Chapter 5
that cross-cultural understanding was possible and we saw in
Chapter 6 that – in the hands of Finnis, Hollis and Chapman – it
was further possible to evaluate differing cultural practices because
the nature of Man constrained the forms that human life could (or
should) take. But perhaps the most significant aspect of this
corollary is the light it sheds on the commonplace, referred to in
Chapter 2, that the idea of human nature is central or intrinsic to

political ideologies and doctrines. It is because, as elaborated in Chapter 7, human nature by distinguishing between the human and the natural worlds serves to define what is political that it has this crucial central status. We will develop this point in Chapter 10.

In conclusion we need perhaps to reiterate that there is no predetermined use to which awareness of these limits can be put. This use can be negative (for example, anarchism is impossible) or positive (for example, human nature can be realised in a true community of Man). In accord with this indeterminacy it is a legitimate exercise to portray an alternative to the status quo. Of course, the alternative vision that is portrayed, whether it be B. F. Skinner's *Walden II*, Plato's *Republic*, Fourier's Phalanstery or whatever, can be criticised for being unrealistic, for flying in the face of human nature. But that is true of all argumentation over human nature and intrinsic to why it is a political issue.

There is, however, a final point. Given that the idea of human nature can be used in this ideal and critical fashion then it does mean that the concept is not necessarily tied to a conservative function. It also means that talk of human nature is not necessarily ideological – in the sense in which I have used the term. We can accept that the notion of human nature imposes limits on human action without accepting that the institutions of the status quo embody these limits.

9 Challenges to Human Nature

The last seven chapters have been devoted to exploring the three posited facets of the concept of human nature. The argument has assumed throughout that the concept is meaningful or intelligible. This assumption, however, can be challenged. In the light of the problems and issues that we have raised two major challenges can be discerned. The first, represented by existentialism, attacks the idea of givenness and the associated idea that human nature can provide a definitive ideal of human flourishing. The second challenge, represented by pragmatism, attacks the idea of human nature as a trans-cultural constant which can provide a universal foundation to render the diversity of human experience commensurable. I have chosen Jean-Paul Sartre to exemplify the existentialist challenge and Richard Rorty to represent the pragmatist one.

Jean-Paul Sartre

The doctrine of existentialism proffers perhaps the best known critique of the notion of 'human nature'. Hannah Arendt for example remarks at the beginning of her stimulating book *The Human Condition* (1958, p.10) that nothing entitles us to assume that Man has a nature or an essence in the same sense as other things. However, it is Sartre who gives the now 'classic' argument here (even if he himself may later have changed his ground) and it is to that argument that Arendt alludes.

The first principle of existentialism according to Sartre is that 'Man is nothing else but that which he makes of himself' (1973, p.28). This principle is not a mere restatement of the potentialist view of human nature discussed in Chapter 8 because it is to be taken in the strongest possible sense. To believe in human nature at all is to believe that there is something outside Man that establishes for Man a 'nature'. To Sartre this 'something' is God. Yet since there is no God it follows that there is no human nature. There are, therefore, with respect to Man, no givens. We define ourselves; we are what we will. The corollary of this absence of 'givens' is that human action cannot be explained as an effect by reference to human nature as a cause. This denial of antecedent causality is a denial of determinism and an affirmation of freedom (p.34). This freedom is not optional but is 'the stuff of my being' (1966, p.566). We cannot escape this freedom. We cannot shrug off our responsibility for our lives by claiming that matters are beyond our control. In particular it is no excuse to say that it is 'only human nature' to do or not to do some action. Freedom is choice and this is inescapable. For Sartre, therefore, human 'being' is synonymous with being free which itself is synonymous with acting.

Two obvious questions present themselves. The first of these is, surely there are limits to freedom? I cannot will myself to see through a brick wall. But Sartre rejoins that limits on freedom are required for there to be freedom. Humans always exist concretely in the world, that is, they exist in a specific 'situation'. This is the paradox of freedom – 'there is freedom only in a situation and there is a situation only through freedom. Human-reality everywhere encounters resistance and obstacles which it has not created, but these resistances and obstacles have meaning only in and through the free choice which human-reality *is*' (1966, p.629: Sartre's emphasis). Sartre proceeds to analyse this 'situation' into the conditions of what he calls human facticity – my place, my past, my environment, my fellow-man, my death. We can illustrate Sartre's meaning by noting briefly what he has to say about the first of these. By 'place' is meant, in the most general sense, the spatial order within which an individual must be found. The individual, however, is not static but actively relates to this place. This relationship is to be understood in terms of the individual's choices. Thus Sartre says that it is in terms of choices that my place can be an aid (I wish to be a wealthy farmer in Mont-de-Marsan) or hindrance (I am not free to go to New York because I am a minor official in Mont-de-Marsan) (1966, pp.629–36).

The second question concerns the apparently ineliminable

capriciousness of human action. Without the guidance of either God or Nature then surely any one human action is as good as any other? As Roquentin, the central character in Sartre's novel *Nausea* (1965), remarks 'everything is gratuitous, that park, this town, and myself' (p.188). Upon becoming aware of this Roquentin contemplates suicide but then realises that if everything is indeed gratuitous then so too is his death. The book ends with Roquentin deciding to write a novel, an act that might give his life a meaning.

The moral is that since there are no external givens then we cannot decide *a priori* what to do but must always choose in terms of our 'project' – our future commitment – and that always takes place within a situation. We have to make a choice whether to join the Resistance against the Nazis or to stay with our widowed mother still grieving the death of her eldest son (1973, p.35). We ought to recognise, 'dread-full' or anguished though such recognition might be, that we have to make a choice and acknowledge our responsibility in so doing. Not to do this is an act of self-deception or 'bad faith' (1966, ch. 2).

How cogent is this (abbreviated) argument for dismissing the concept of human nature? Mary Midgely for one sees little or no cogency in it. She proclaims that the existentialist doctrine that we create ourselves out of nothing just 'does not make sense' (1978, p.xx). This proclamation, however, rests on Midgley's own argument that humans do have a nature and on a certain robust commonsense, both of which could be construed as begging the question.

The most obvious objection to Sartre is to observe that his saying Man has no essence commits him to a universalism: *all* humans it would seem are essentially free. There is a danger here of confusing necessary and sufficient conditions. Whilst universality may well be a necessary condition of a concept of human nature it is not of itself a sufficient condition. As we have stressed in this book, human nature has facets or dimensions. Yet, in fact, Sartre does use universalist language, talking not of 'human nature' but of the 'human condition'. Significantly from that universalist premise Sartre declares that no human purpose is foreign; a European can understand a Chinaman. That this is so is seemingly in virtue of the universality that 'every purpose is comprehensible to every man' (1973, p.46). Sartre reiterates that this universality is not a given but is made by, for example, understanding another's purposes.

However, Sartre does not allow that these purposes can be just anything. He does allow for the constants of 'being in the world, of having to labour and die there' (ibid). It would now seem to follow that it is these universal constants which permit this comprehension of others. But such constants are now suggestive of another facet of human nature – its givenness. It is an integral part of Sartre's own system to distinguish between what he calls 'being-in-itself' and 'being-for-itself'. The former is 'opaque', that is to say it refers to things where appearance and reality are identical. Thanks to this identity being-in-itself is never anything other than what it is (1966, pp.28–9). The latter lacks this identity. There is a gap, so to speak, between appearance and reality and this gap Sartre calls 'nothingness'. But nothingness, Sartre is clear, is the prerogative of human consciousness. One of his own examples might make this clearer: 'of this table I can say only that it is purely and simply *this* table. But I cannot limit myself to saying that my belief is belief; [because] my belief is the consciousness of belief' (1966, p.121: Sartre's emphasis). Although my belief and my consciousness of belief are inseparable yet they are not identical, there is a gap (or nothingness) between them. Human consciousness, the for-itself, therefore, always exists at a distance to itself and thus always determines itself to exist (1966, p.126). Stones just exist (as a being-for-itself a stone is a stone is a stone) humans decide to exist. Accordingly, the supposed truism that Man is not a stone lies at the heart of Sartre's philosophy and, as such, the category of human-ness constitutes its very core. Nor is the facet of practicality absent from this thought. Sartre does have a conception of how humans ought to live; to live a life of bad faith is to live a less than fully human life. Indeed, Sartre closes *Being and Nothingness* with a discussion of the ethical implications of his argument. In that discussion he outlines the idea of an existentialist psychoanalysis. This enterprise he defines as a 'moral description' which 'is going to reveal to man the real goal of his pursuit'. This goal is that Man is free and the unique source of value (1966, p.797). Possessed with this knowledge Man can (perhaps) overcome the first act of bad faith, namely, 'to flee what it cannot flee, to flee what it is' (1966, p.115).

The upshot of this discussion is that it is not a distortion to hold that Sartre's idea of human-ness incorporates our three facets of the concept of human nature – practicality, universality and givenness.

In view of this it would appear that the work of the concept is still being done merely under another label and he has not, in effect, dispensed with it. It is an act of stipulation on Sartre's part to dismiss the concept of 'human nature'. In other words, since he attributes to this term a very specific stipulative meaning he is thus unable to acknowledge the concept's presence in his thought under that label.

Richard Rorty

Rorty is an iconoclast. He wants to break the idols of traditional philosophy. In particular he criticises its pretensions to provide the touchstone by which the nature of reality can be known. Traditionally philosophers aimed to establish the foundations of knowledge. Once these foundations have been established then philosophers will possess the definitive or 'final vocabulary' (1982, p.xlii). This vocabulary will then be employed to judge all other vocabularies or ways of describing reality. It will distinguish between those vocabularies that represent reality well and those that perform that task less well or even not at all (1980, pp.3, 269). In this way philosophy adjudicates between the claims (vocabularies) of, say, astrology and astronomy to tell the truth about the nature of reality.

In place of these pretensions Rorty proffers the claims of pragmatism. The essence of pragmatism is that there is no effective difference between the propositions (i) 'it works because it is true' and (ii) 'it is true because it works' (1982, p.xxix). What has this to do with human nature?

Rorty sees merit in Sartre's emphasis on the priority of existence over essence. As Rorty interprets him Sartre is 'making the point that man is always free to choose new descriptions' (1980, p.362n). Since for the pragmatist there is no reality that thought is supposed to mirror – only different ways of coping with the world via the vocabularies at our disposal – there are no privileged descriptions of human nature. We can gloss this point by observing that it means that the work of scientists like E. O. Wilson, notwithstanding the broad neo-Darwinian consensus within which they operate, is of itself no more revelatory of human nature than 'the various alternative descriptions offered by poets, novelists, depth-psychologists, sculptors, anthropologists and mystics' (1980, p.362). The work of such individuals is all part of the repertoire of self-descriptions available. In some circumstances (to gloss once more) one vocabulary will seem appropriate – the biochemical language of chromosomes for sexual identity, for example – and in other circumstances, another vocabulary – the language of action and purpose for legal responsibility, for example. The criterion of appropriateness is utility (1982, pp.153, 197).

To believe that there is an essential human nature is to believe, like the universalists who we discussed in Chapters 4, 5, and 6, that there is one possible description of Man that renders all possible descriptions commensurable (1980, p.378). This description would depict Man as he 'really' is. To Rorty, however, these universalists are subscribing to the seventeenth-century myth of Nature's Own Vocabulary. According to this myth Galileo's philosophy worked because he correctly described the way things really were. In contrast Rorty claims that Galileo just 'lucked out' by having a better idea and more helpful terminology about motion than Aristotle (1982, p.193).

But if there is no underlying nature of Man what is there? What is there is what 'we' put there through our past vocabularies – 'there is nothing deep down inside us except what we have put there ourselves, no criterion that we have not created in the course of creating a practice, no standard of rationality that is not an appeal to such a criterion, no rigorous argumentation that is not obedience to our own conventions' (1982, p.xiii). Where does that leave us? If Man can be known only under 'optional descriptions' (1980, p.379) then which of these is chosen will depend on the choosers and their purposes; 'we simply cast around for a vocabulary which lets us get what we want' (1982, p.52). The outcome of this would appear to be that since, for example, Marx wants revolution he describes Man as a maker of history (1977, p.300). This vocabulary will enable Marx to establish the transience of capitalism – it is a historical product – and the practical possibility of its supersession by socialism because what Man has made can be unmade. But it is equally the outcome that since Augustine wants to disentangle the mundane fate of the Roman Empire from the spiritual purpose of Christianity he describes Man as a being in but not of this world (cf. 1945, vol. 2, p.255). This vocabulary will enable Augustine to establish the comparative futility of investing in temporal glory when set against the vouchsafed beatitude of eternal peace in the life hereafter.

Rorty's argument is that despite what theorists think they are doing they are in fact merely manipulating vocabularies. Thus although both Marx and Augustine do here employ what is in their eyes a definitive concept of Man (it is practical, universal and a given) for Rorty this is a mistake – the notion of human nature has no useful work to do.

However, as with Sartre, this derives from his own particular preoccupations. Rorty's aim is to replace an essentially Platonic and Kantian way of Philosophising (*sic*) and he identifies the idea of 'Man' as belonging to that 'way'. Given this preoccupation Rorty's argument could be sidestepped simply by disputing that the idea of human nature has necessarily to be located within this Kantian approach. Nevertheless, for the purposes of argument, we can challenge his view in more positive terms. While it might seem plausible to reject Rorty's interpretation of Galileo's superiority over Aristotle by remarking that the reason why Galileo 'copes' is because he, rather than Aristotle, expresses the reality about motion, the argument regarding Man is perhaps less plausibly rejected given the concept's practical rather theoretical character. The nub point therefore becomes whether Rorty himself successfully copes without a concept of Man. Can he pass his own pragmatic test?

His discussion of human solidarity or community provides an arena for this assessment. Rorty judges that bourgeois liberalism is the best example of this solidarity and that pragmatism is the best articulation of it. These judgments follow the remark that liberalism does not require the support of a notion of a common human nature but does require a sense of community (1982, p.207). This appears to mean that although 'human nature' has no work to do in upholding liberalism, the notion of community is functional. Pragmatism, of the sort Rorty attributes to Dewey, can now enter the scene to provide the hope of a renewed sense of community, 'our identification with our community – our society, our political tradition, our intellectual heritage – is heightened when we see this community as *ours* rather than *nature's*, *shaped* rather than *found*, one among the many which men have made' (1982, p.166, Rorty's emphases).

The last phrase raises doubts as to whom the 'our' in the quotation refers. In one place Rorty declares that anthropologists have enabled we Westerners to see any exotic specimen of humanity as 'one of us' (1982, p.201). This seems to imply that, after all, some standard notion of human nature does have some work to do by rendering this identification possible. But Rorty elsewhere apparently denies this by stating that pragmatism must remain ethnocentric (1982, p.173). We can only apply our, Western, criteria of relevance. The implication of this is that for non-Westerners to be 'one of us' does not entail that 'we are one of them'. The reason Rorty does not regard this as a drawback is because 'loyalty to our fellow-humans' does not require 'something permanent and unhistorical . . . which guarantees convergence to agreement' (1982, p.171). It is seemingly sufficient that this pragmatic perspective enjoins us Westerners to solidarity with others. It is the presence of this injunction that presumably gives liberalism its superiority. However, this superiority is at the cost of simply brushing aside any problems about identifying non-Westerners as human. We 'simply' take up a certain point of view of our fellow humans (1982, p.202). More drastically, we can, on Rorty's version of liberalism, also brush away a culture's explanation of its own social practices as 'primitive' or 'nutty' (1982, p.200; cf. 1980, p.352). Such a dismissal is apparently without prejudice to our solidarity with them because 'pragmatists tell us what matters is our loyalty to other human beings' (1982, p.166).

Whether Rorty's pragmatic case for this solidarity is convincing without some notion of human nature is doubtful. But even if his ethnocentrism is granted there still remains an area of doubt, namely, it is unclear how he can justify the coherence that he must presume to exist when he refers to the 'West'. In reply to a hypothetical challenge to his ethnocentrism he states:

> 'the pragmatist cannot answer the question "What is so special about Europe?" save by saying "Do you have anything non-European to suggest which meets *our* European purposes better?" He cannot answer the question "What is so good about the Socratic virtues, abut Miltonic free encounters, about undistorted communication?" save by saying "What else would better fulfil the purposes *we* share with Socrates, Milton and Habermas?" ' (1982, p.174: Rorty's emphases)

Rorty takes it for granted that 'we' do share these purposes. He puts forward without any real argument a historicist thesis – '*we* are the people who have read and pondered Plato, Newton, Kant, Marx, Darwin, Freud, Dewey etc.' (1982, p.173: Rorty's emphasis). The pragmatist is now said to hold along with Hegel that 'truth and justice lie in the direction marked by successive stages of European thought' (ibid).

There are two comments to be made about this. Firstly, Rorty judges that this direction culminates in Dewey rather than Marx. He is explicit that 'bourgeois capitalist society' is the 'best polity actualised so far' (1982, p.210) and that Marx's view of the proletariat as the 'Redeemed Form of Man' 'has to go' (1982, p.207). But by 'best' all Rorty can mean is 'copes with most satisfactorily' yet by what criterion that judgment is to be made is left unspoken. What Rorty does say is that this 'best polity' is 'irrelevant to most of the problems of the population of the planet' (1982, p.210). This means not only denying that Marxist vocabulary is any more relevant but also implies that these 'problems' are beyond coping with.

Secondly, Rorty's relationship to Hegel is ambiguous. On the one hand he wants to preserve the Hegelian idea of understanding philosophy historically. (Rorty thinks of the history of philosophy as a continuing conversation (1980, pp.389ff)). On the other hand he wants to reject the Hegelian framework. However, these two desires appear to be incompatible. If, like Rorty, we accept Hegel's historicist argument that the 'present' is constituted by the 'past'; that we today incorporate in our world-view the views of past generations then we are committed with Hegel to postulating a common Spirit or some conceptual equivalent in which we are all participants. Without that commitment there is no way that we can regard the past as in any sense 'ours'. Rorty, nevertheless, reneges on that commitment.

He is explicit that Hegel's idea of Man 'has to go' (1982, p.217). In its place he, presumably like Dewey, wants 'man's history' to be unadorned with any notion of Absolute Spirit (1982, p.47). Yet it is this rejection that leaves his historicism problematic. It is unclear how we are to know that *this* history is that 'of man' unless some notion of an enduring subject (Man) is being presupposed. The point here is that Rorty is rejecting too much. In getting rid of the (Kantian) assumption that there must be a grounding or ultimate agreement in the conversation he is also getting rid of the source of his confidence that we are participants in the same conversations –

that we are indeed able to talk together about these postulated shared purposes. Once again, therefore, it is doubtful if Rorty's pragmatic case for liberalism is tenable without relying on some (orthodox) notion of human nature.

The general, if perhaps unfairly brutal, upshot of this discussion is that either Rorty's pragmatic historicism does retain in its operating principles a recognisable view of human nature, so that the notion has not been jettisoned, or, if it has been jettisoned, then pragmatism turns into a variant of relativism and, since relativism fails the pragmatic test of utility because, as we saw in Chapter 5, the relativist is strictly precluded from saying anything constructive, then Rorty's argument need not be heeded.

Both Sartre and Rorty claim that the idea of human nature is dispensable. For Sartre this idea implied that Man was a thing (like a stone) that could be known from 'outside'. But, as Arendt puts it, this 'would be like jumping over our own shadows' (p.10) because Man has no 'outside' in the same sense that a stone has. For Rorty this idea belonged to a mistaken tradition of thought which sought to uncover 'reality' or the basic foundation of true knowledge. The validity of both the existentialist and pragmatist treatments of the concept of human nature stem from their own very particular premises. Yet even aside from the disputability of these premises their arguments are not wholly convincing. Regarding both positions a case can be made to show that 'human nature' is dispensed with in name only and that, in effect, the concept remains. We will consider why the concept of human nature appears to be indispensable in our final chapter.

10   Human Nature and Politics

Politics as an activity is inseparable from values. No matter how much it concerns itself with supposed technical administrative and bureaucratic issues these 'means' can never be entirely divorced from questions of 'ends'. These 'ends' are always related to human purposes and aims – why be 'efficient'? Why does it matter how 'big' government is? It is this relationship that explains why at the beginning of Chapter 2 it was stated that politics was a branch of ethics. Hence terms like power, responsibility, rights, freedom, justice and so on are ineliminable from politics. The question now is, how – if at all – does human nature fit into the picture? How does human nature matter to or in politics?

The short answer to this question is that human nature matters politically because of the concept is both indispensable and contentious. Clearly we need to expand upon this answer.

It is part of the motivating interest of theorists of human nature to tell 'how it is': Man is a political animal, is a communal producer, is proud, is adapted to Ice-Age circumstances and so on and on. (It is, in fact, a common criticism of Rorty's pragmatism that he can provide no rationale for the continuance of that motivation). But why do these theorists have this motivating interest? They have it because the comprehension of the nature of Man provides them with a definition of the human world. Since politics is an apparently ineliminable element of that world, it too is established by human nature. Put this way it is not conceivable that a theory of human nature could ever become redundant. Politics howsoever it is defined is at least about human relationships – it is neither about billiard-balls colliding nor hens pecking.

We do, however, have to be more precise about the way that politics may be said to be 'established' by human nature. That human nature seems inseparable from politics, does not mean that the relationship between the two is straightforwardly deductive with human nature necessarily serving as a premise to a political conclusion. The relationship is less direct. The nature of Man acts as a presupposition. What a theory of human nature establishes is what can count as a premise to a political conclusion. In other words it establishes presuppositionally the area, field or conceptual space within which politics operates. As an example of this recall E. O. Wilson's judgment that the findings of sociobiology make anarchism impossible. Furthermore since this field is, as this example bears out, intimately connected with values then human nature can also be said to operate as a metaethic (cf. McShea, 1978, p.675).

The determination of this field realises two objectives or ends which together constitute the indispensability of the concept of human nature. Firstly, to repeat the point just made, it procures for each theory of human nature a reading of the human world within which context political prescriptions can be located. Secondly, and simultaneously, it provides each theory with an authoritative context (an ideal) in terms of which other prescriptions can be dismissed as unrealistic or not worthy of being taken seriously. In telling 'how it is' a theory of human nature is thus not only staking out the field within which political issues can arise, it is, in doing this, also claiming that field for its own and applying it to other theories. It aims to preempt the conceptual space and thus situate *all* accounts in *its* territory. For example, for Augustine, Man is a sinner and since, on Augustine's interpretation, an expression of this sinfulness is the desire to rule (*libido dominandi*) then notions of harmonious co-operation are no more than pipedreams – to ignore this fact of human nature is to produce a worthless political doctrine; all theories if they are to be taken seriously must come to terms with this fact. It is this combination of positive and negative ends – making a case and preempting critics of it – that underlies the commonplace that the idea of human nature is central or intrinsic (and hence indispensable) to the formulation of political doctrines and ideologies.

Implicit in this discussion of the concept's indispensability is its associated status – its contentiousness. We can bring out this contentiousness initially by making an illustrative parallel with Hobbes's notion of 'glory' (1914, p.64). Hobbes used 'glory' to make watertight his argument for the nastiness of the State of Nature. To adapt the proverb, in Hobbes's interpretation each and every man wants to be 'chief' and simultaneously wants everybody else to be 'indians'. Accordingly as a matter of logic – rather than a consequence of conceivably contingent facts like competition over scarce material goods – conflict is now assured. Analogously accounts of human nature claim chiefdom over the field of human conduct and they cannot, as accounts of human nature, tolerate other chiefs; they thus seek to make them indians. But since the upshot of this is to have 'all chiefs' and 'no indians' then the claim made by every theory of human nature to preempt all others guarantees that the articulation of a theory of human nature will – like Hobbes's State of Nature – be a contentious matter.

This contentiousness is thus not incidental to theorising about human nature. This conclusion is to be expected given, firstly, the connexion, maintained throughout this study, between the phenomenon of politics and argument or dispute and given, secondly, the way in which a theory of human nature stakes out the space within which politics takes place. To invoke human nature is to claim that one form of life is superior to another. As we noted when discussing the ideality of human nature in Chapter 2, this can take on both positive and negative forms. Positively this form is expressed in, for example, Marx's vision of communism and negatively it is expressed in any view which holds that, for example, systematic female infanticide is a perverted, 'unnatural', social practice. The concept of human nature thus serves to reject both relativism and the ethical formalism of writers like R. M. Hare. The essential claim that is central to both these rejections is that human nature is not completely indeterminate. If a concept of human nature is indispensable then it means that a view of the good life is inescapable. But since this indispensability of the idea of human nature goes hand in hand with its contentiousness then it means that no vision of the good life is logically compelling. This is why it is always possible to deny the prescriptive import of any particular descriptive depiction of the facts of human nature.

The consequence of this is that the space staked out by a theory of human nature is not coercive; it does not of itself determine assent. A theorist who sees Man as a co-operative being will not acquiesce in Augustine's depiction of Man's *libido dominandi* as a statement of 'how it is'. In effect this means rejecting the field that Augustine has staked out. This 'staking out' is the principal work of the facets of universality and givenness (for Augustine, all humans are sinners and this is a condition outside their control) but, aside from any considerations of the underdetermination of theories by facts, the facet of practicality ensures that what is identified as a universal given is open to challenge; recall that the truths of practice are 'capable of being otherwise'. Facts are judged to be facts of *human nature* (and not merely statements that happen to refer to human beings) in virtue of the work they do in establishing grounds for action in the human world. It follows that Glendon Schubert is being presumptuous when he claims that biological and related theory is going 'to jack political philosophy off its classical presumptions', whether these be the view that political theory began with Socrates or the view that 'naturalistic fables', like those of Hobbes and Rousseau, can constitute a viable understanding of the roots of political behaviour (1976, p.164). It is not necessarily obscurantist, let alone anti-scientific, to accept on the one hand neo-Darwinism and to deny on the other hand its relevance to (say) deciding what is the just state. It is too easy to jump from the premise that Man is a creature of natural selection to the conclusion that this fact *must* therefore be politically relevant. This jump is precisely the preemptive strike identified above as the negative objective in staking out the field.

It is this same preemptiveness that explains why the idea of human nature figures so prominently in ideological argumentation. This prominence is due precisely to its field-staking or presuppositional role in determining the appropriate ground for human action. One person's explanation is another's justification. Barash's sociobiological explanation of sexual double standards is to his critics a justification of capitalist sexist practices.

Here we can see an illustration of how this twin status of indispensability and contentiousness accounts for the shaky reputation that the notion of 'human nature' now enjoys. On what can be loosely termed the ideological Right, writers like J. L. Talmon (1970, Introd.) imply that the belief (of the Left) that real interests can be imputed to human nature without specific human individuals necessarily being aware of these interests undermines a free society and underpins a dictatorship in the name (merely) of the people. On the ideological Left, writers like Robert Young, whom we discussed in Chapter 8, take the view that the claim (of the Right) that some institutions reflect permanent realities of human nature is an obstructive and obfuscatory myth and, as such, a hindrance to social change. Furthermore, as we noted in Chapter 6, due in no small measure to this distrust, there has been a tendency in political literature either to drop all explicit references to human nature or to attempt to confine statements about human nature to (hoped for) generally acceptable formal attributes.

To summarise some salient aspects of this book's overall argument I shall use some arguments of Stuart Hampshire because he is one writer who, though in a different context, puts forward a case for both the indispensability of a concept of Man and a recognition of its contentiousness.

Hampshire remarks that the grounds by which a thinker distinguishes politics from other human activities are disputable and commit that thinker to a number of consequences in the application of other disputable concepts (1965, p.231). Central to these ramifying consequences is the concept of Man and it is from the perspective of *that* concept that other disputed notions '*must* fall into place' (p.232: my emphasis). The concept of Man thus assumes a privileged place. Indeed, Hampshire goes so far as to state 'it is possible to characterise philosophy itself as a search for a "definition of man" and to interpret the great philosophers of the past as each providing a different account of the powers essential to man' (p.232). While thinkers like Aristotle may have thought the concept of Man was definitively ascertainable, Hampshire believes that today such confidence is no longer possible. Instead we have to settle for a depiction of human nature (though Hampshire himself never uses that phrase) as a 'reasoned proposal' that emanates from a philosophy of mind. This philosophy however will be disputable as will the emanation from it: it is a matter of 'opinion' not 'demonstration' (in our terms, it is a matter of 'practice' not 'theory').

Hampshire goes on to explain how it is that the concept of Man is so central. Echoing the argument for the universalism of human nature given in Chapters 4 and 5, Hampshire claims that there exists a number of 'permanent and distinctive' conditions that must characterise human life and which are 'the necessary basis of the comparison between men of different periods and cultures' (p.237).

Echoing the argument for the duality of human nature given in Chapter 2, Hampshire claims that investigation into what is valuable necessarily invokes human interests, 'however resolutely we may try, as philosophers, to separate judgments of value from any limiting human interests we can never altogether succeed. The human interests are included in the formation of the concepts to which the evaluative epithets are attached' (p.258). There is an ineliminable anthropocentrism involved in making ultimate judgments of value. This applies even to Plato's explicitly supernatural reality of Forms or even to purely natural processes like perhaps Shaw's celebration of the life-force in *Don Juan in Hell* (Hampshire himself cites the writings of D. H. Lawrence as an example). Echoing the argument for the necessity of limits given in Chapters 7 and 8, Hampshire declares that every question of morality and public policy must necessarily be confined by ideas about what men are or can be. But these questions do not always arise in the same form. To give Hampshire's own example; an Aristotelian would assess governments by the extent to which they produced conditions in which essential human excellencies are attainable, whilst a utilitarian would not refer to essential virtues but instead assess political decisions by their efficiency in preserving states of mind that are independently known to be good (pp.262–3). The difference here is more than a difference in terminology and, because of that, there is no necessity that the disputants would even agree as to where and in what their disagreement lies. Such a disagreement is what Hampshire means by a disagreement in opinion. These disagreements are always corrigible and thus there is always a need to give supporting reasons for the position taken up and a commitment to reconsider the position if the reasons are shown to be indefensible (p.264).

Although his aims are different from ours Hampshire's argument bears out a basic message of this book: there is nothing self-evident about the nature of human nature. Judgments about human nature are concept-dependent. To re-utilise two examples from earlier discussion, what Burke and Freud conceptualise as the 'stuff' of human nature differs just as Marx and Augustine differ, and each of these four differs also from the other three. This state of affairs prompts a final question: are there ways to adjudicate between them?

There can be no definitive answer to the question, 'what is human nature?' The question is essentially open-ended. As we have argued the role actually performed by the concept of human nature in political theory is demarcational and presuppositional. This explains, firstly, how debate on straightforwardly political issues like justice and democracy can, as sketched out in Chapter 1, be pushed back into competing views of human nature and, secondly, it explains how, because of its role in determining the field within which politics can take place, this competition cannot be resolved by reference to the issue being contested. Does this mean that debate over human nature is therefore unresolvable?

At the risk of appearing quixotic the answer to this question is – 'given human nature, yes'. But it does not follow from the fact that there can be no final definitive answer that no criticism is possible or that one argument cannot be judged to be overall preferable to or better than another. There are criteria available to permit reasoned choice between them. We can mention two candidates.

One, is a theory internally consistent? Sociobiology and other 'scientific' accounts are frequently seen as weak on this score. Oakeshott sums up the germ of the weakness in a typically ironic footnote:

'When a geneticist tells us "all social behaviour and historical events are the inescapable consequences of the genetic individuality of the persons concerned" we have no difficulty in recognizing this theorem as a brilliant illumination of the writings of Aristotle, the fall of Constantinople, the deliberations of the House of Commons on Home Rule for Ireland and the death of Barbarosa; but this brilliance is, perhaps, somewhat dimmed when it becomes clear that he can have nothing more revealing to say about his science of genetics than that it also is *all* done by genes, and that this theorem is itself his genes speaking.' (1975, p.15n: Oakeshott's emphasis)

More mundanely the charge is that such accounts want the best of both worlds. They want, on the one hand, to say that Man is a product of an evolutionary genetic history or operant-conditioning yet they hold, on the other hand, that writing books about this to be read by others can make a difference. By indulging in the latter enterprise both Wilson and Skinner, for example, are committing themselves to reflecting upon the validity of their scientific conclusions. But this very reflectiveness means that they are convinced by the validity of their science and not by their being genetically programmed or operantly conditioned into saying what they do say. Similarly, they believe it is this validity that will persuade their readers and not the fact that their readers are biologically or behaviouristically determined to accept their arguments. The question of how we come to hold as true that which we do as a matter of fact hold to be true is a separate question from the truth of what is held. To confuse these questions is to render void the endeavour to supply a scientific account of Man. In sum, any adequate theory of human nature must be reflexive, it must apply to the very act itself of theorising about human nature. And to speak crudely, neither genes nor pigeons read or write books.

A second criterion by which to assess a theory of human nature is whether it adequately accommodates the 'facts'. Does the theory in staking out the field and preempting thereby its rivals satisfactorily accommodate the 'facts' these rivals deem significant? In other words we can ask whether the comprehensiveness that a theory claims for itself subjects that theory to too great an internal strain so that it loses inner coherence. This element of inner coherence provides some perspective by which to see if a particular concept of human nature coheres overall relatively well or relatively ill.

Thus, for example, Aristotle's contemplative account might be judged less coherent than Marx's when the feelings of solidarity that come from working together are considered. Or again Hobbes's view that the avoidance of death is the chief impulsion in human life coheres less well than Seneca's appraisal of the worth of life when the rates and reasons for suicide are borne in mind. Or, to take a third and final example, Godwin's belief that suitably educated individuals will see that justice is no respecter of persons can be judged inadequate when set against the findings of sociobiology that humans act so as best to maximise their inclusive genetic fitness. The point in these examples is not that Aristotle, Hobbes and Godwin are contradicting themselves. Aristotle would not deny that humans get satisfaction from working together, Hobbes would not deny suicides take place and Godwin would not deny the emotional preference of a parent for its own child. Rather, the point is that in their attempt to determine the field, to accommodate preemptively rival views, these three can be judged to have over-reached themselves. Accordingly, Aristotle's argument that co-operative labour is in truth an impediment to free activity can be assessed as forced or contrived. Similarly, Hobbes's argument that suicide is an act of (temporary) madness and Godwin's argument that parental affections are a transient imperfection can both be assessed as forced. These strains in their accounts can be judged unreasonable. The theorists can be interpreted as buying consistency at the too great a cost of sacrificing plausibility and thus their accounts *can* be passed over in favour of another.

Adjudication is thus possible even if there is no definitive answer. What final conclusion can be drawn? The most sensible would be that we should not expect too much from a concept of human nature. It can be used with profit diagnostically to see what makes a political theory 'tick' but we should not hope to think that we can articulate a view which will solve political problems or dissolve political issues. That is too much to ask if only because the theory itself is part of the 'problem' and constitutive of the 'issue'. Indeed a self-denying ordinance is in order. Knowing that recourse to human nature is not going to end dispute then it should not pretend to that role. One can certainly ask of theorists what view of Man is held and ask that they be clear what that view is and what they think follows from it. But no theorist should think that articulating a view of Man is going to disarm criticism and no critic should think that rejecting a view of Man renders at a stroke a political theory void, for the critic is also a theorist to whom the same principle applies.

If nothing else, the foregoing pages should have served to throw into question the common practice of referring to 'human nature' as a definitional and argumentational stop. To invoke human nature will not end debate, it is more likely to start one; after all, that's human nature for you!

Guide to Further Reading

This survey is divided into two parts. In the first I make some observations on the literature relevant to the general topic that this book covers and in the second I supply some indications of literature that I have drawn upon in my own argument and to some of the complementary literature on the main themes discussed.

I

For a topic as broad as Human Nature and Politics there are surprisingly few books explicitly devoted to it. The topic does have its 'classic' text in Graham Wallas's *Human Nature in Politics* (1924 – first edition 1908) but this is designed to correct what he termed the 'intellectualist assumption' that every human action was the product of deliberation and to advocate, in its stead, that attention should be paid to the findings of psychology which have brought out the importance of non-rational factors in human life. In his own way therefore Wallas's book is to be judged (alongside W. Bagehot's *Physics and Politics* (n.d. written 1867–72)) as a forerunner, in principle, of contemporary exponents of the need to make politics conform to the findings of Science.

There are two useful collections of essays, one edited by Pennock and Chapman (1977) the other by Forbes and Smith (1983). The former volume contains an extensive bibliography. As with most collections of this sort the contents are diverse, dealing (though the Forbes and Smith collection rather more systematically) with individual topics or aspects.

Surveys of the broader topic of human nature are also provided by collections: Benthall (1973) which contains significant essays by Casey and Young; Platt (1965) which includes Geertz's important essay on the relationship between Culture and Man; Rothblatt (1968) which includes essays by Chomsky, Dobzhansky and a distinguished contribution from McKeon. An issue of *Social Research* (vol. 40, 1973) devoted to human nature provides a snapshot of the variety of concerns and approaches that the subject both invites and accommodates. Leslie Stevenson has written a clear brief introductory monography, *Seven Theories of Human Nature* (1974), which provides extremely succint summaries of Plato, Christianity, Marx, Feud, Sartre, Skinner and Lorenz and analyses them in a common

141

framework. This volume has been supplemented by a book of readings, *The Study of Human Naure* (1981) which ranges from the Old Testament and the Upanishads to Wilson and Habermas. Another book of readings is supplied by Fromm and Xirau, *The Nature of Man* (1968), but whilst equally far-ranging suffers from the general brevity of the extracts chosen. Though far less introductory than Stevenson's book, Mary Midgley's *Beast and Man* (1978) provides a lively defence of the idea of human nature and is critically sympathetic of the work of ethologists like Eibl-Eibesfeldt.

While there is thus not an abundance of volumes on the broad topic there are many studies of the place of the concept of human nature in the thought of individual theorists; for example, Geras (1983) on Marx, Clark (1975) on Aristotle, Berry (1982) on Hume and Hegel. There are also studies that use the idea of human nature as a motif to explore the thought of an age or movement; for example, Adkins (1970) on the Greeks, Crocker (1959) on the Enlightenment, Heller (1978) on the Renaissance and Gaus (1983) on modern liberalism. While all of these studies are valuable they do not subject the concept of human nature itself to any extensive analysis.

II

In this section I take up in rough order of treatment the major topics covered in my own analysis of the concept's three facets.

Practicality

The idea of the conceptual dependence of facts is well-established. Hilary Putnam's (1981) essays provide a relatively accessible way into what does become a complicated area. Mary Hesse's (1980) essays also survey in a broad and challenging way the issues raised. In the context of political science a polemical utilisation of this idea against logical positivism and empiricism is given by Gunnell (1975). The literature on ethical naturalism is perhaps best approached through articles collected in either *The Definition of Morality* edited by Wallace and Walker (1970) – this contains Foot's article 'Moral Arguments' as well as Anscombe's influential 'Modern Moral Philosophy' – or in *Theories of Ethics* edited by Foot (1967) which contains her own 'Moral Beliefs' together with relevant contributions from Frankena, Searle and Hare. Bernard Williams's (1972) introductory book to moral philosophy touches most appositely and clearly on the general concerns raised by the discussion. My own formulation of the duality of the concept of human nature has been influenced by Julius Kovesi's *Moral Notions* (1967).

Universality

Most histories of thought deal with Natural Law. D'Entrèves's (1951) account is simple and straightforward; more advanced but more rewarding is R. Tuck's *Natural Rights Theory* (1979). On the relationship between *physis* and *nomos* in Greek thought Myres (1927) is informative. A good though not elementary account of Stoicism in general is provided by J. M. Rist (1969). I explore contextualism as a historical doctrine more thoroughly in my 1982 study. The development of contextualism into a view of Man as a symbolic/cultural creature is best exhibited in the work of Ernst Cassirer and most accessibly in his *Essay on Man* (1944). An interesting adaption of Cassirer's work in political theory is Gunnell's *Political Philosophy and Time* (1968) and Tudor (1972) has written a good study of political myth in which Cassirer's work figures prominently. With a more empirical orientation Edelman (e.g. 1971) has made the idea of Man as a symbolic being the centre of his study of political perceptions and actions. As the text indicates Geertz's work (1972) is the best contemporary anthropological version of contextualism. The general question of relativism is best approached through Hollis and Lukes's edited collection (1982) while the earlier volume edited by Wilson (1970) on a similar theme remains useful and includes two pieces by Winch.

Givenness

There are many volumes which outline the mainstream neo-Darwinian position. Dawkins (1976) not only does that imaginatively but also provides a case-study in the possibilities and acknowledged limitations of the application of genetic theory to humans. Much of the recent writing on Human Nature has been on or about what I call Scientific Man, with the ideas of sociobiology at the forefront of a rapidly increasing literature. Once again collections of essays give the best rounded introduction. Montague's collection (1980) supplies a generally hostile view of sociobiology as does, in the main, a special issue of *The Philosophical Forum* volume 13 (1981–82) though this is a good source for further reading. A more balanced collection is offered by Gregory *et al.* (1978) which includes not only a short piece by Wilson himself and a contribution by Barash but also good critical contributions from, amongst others, Washburn, Searle and Schneewind. A simple straightforward non-partisan account of sociobiology is given by Breuer (1982). Philosophically critical accounts yet not without some sympathy are provided by Trigg (1982) and Singer (1981). A thoroughly sympathetic account while not devoid of criticism and which mingles 'biology' and 'philosophy' is von Schilcher and Tennant (1983). The connexions between biology and politics are the concern of a specialist section of the International Political Science Association. Somit (1976) has edited a collection of conference papers which includes not only essays by many of the leading scholars in this field such as Corning, Masters and Davies but which also has much bibliographical information. There is a more recent collection (in German) edited by Flohr and Tönnesmann (1983) with a number of the same authors contributing and where sociobiology, virtually absent from the first volume, has had more impact. Mackenzie (1978) has published a brief book which takes a relaxed and typically synoptic view of the subject. The topic of ideology is a minefield and the literature voluminous. My own use of the term as a pejorative one I take to be in line with an aspect of Marx's treatment. A somewhat breathless and overcompressed survey of the topic is given by Larrain (1979) and Plamenatz's little volume (1971) retains its value as an accessible introduction. The concerns that animate the difficult writings of the Frankfurt School can be helpfully approached via Fay's (1975) monograph. Young's writings (1971, 1973a, 1973b) provide, within the context of 'Science', the best critical account of human nature theory from a Marxist point of view. The work of Rose, Kamin and Lewontin (1984) provides an excellent illustration of the themes discussed in Chapters 7 and 8. While this book, like others of its kind, is savage in its criticisms of the competence of scientific research, it itself proceeds serenely to produce historical generalisations without heeding the specialist literature that would qualify almost every statement they make. One would expect 'human nature' to loom large in feminist theory but its practitioners have tended to concentrate on internal debates. Though not free from this characteristic, Jaggar's (1983) large volume provides an overview along with her own (Marxist) perspective. Briefer accounts are supplied by Ruth Levitas in Forbes and Smith (1983) and by Joan Smith in *The Philosophical Forum* (1982). Holmstrom (1982, 1984) intelligently discusses the vexed issue of whether women have a distinct 'nature'.

Chapters 9 and 10

There is an extensive literature on existentialism. Barrett (1962) has written a general historical and background survey and Sartre has been the subject of several general studies but discussions that focus on his view (or lack of) of human nature are given in Stevenson (1974) and Trigg (1982) and a simple account is given in Nott (1970). The best way into Rorty is via his Introduction to *Consequences of Pragmatism* (1982). Rorty synthesises many recent trends in philosophy, for a general critique of these see Trigg (1980). For the view that seemingly unresolvable contentiousness does not render criticism void see Putnam (1981) or Popper's essay 'On the status of Science and Metaphysics' in his *Conjectures and Refutations* (1968). I should, perhaps, add that I have deliberately foresworn the idiom of 'essential contestability' because, aside from any doubts about its own general and seemingly self-defeating contestability, in the specific case of human nature, I believe it to be superfluous.

Bibliography

Adkins, A. W. D. (1970) *From the Many to the One: A Study of Personality and Human Nature in the Context of Ancient Greek Society, Values and Beliefs* (Ithaca, NY: Cornell University Press).

Alpers, J. (1978) 'Ethical and social implications', in M. Gregory, A. Silvers and D. Sutch (eds), *Sociobiology and Human Nature* (San Francisco: Jossey Bass) pp.195–211.

Apel, K. O. (1979) 'Towards a reconstruction of Critical Theory', in S. C Brown (ed.), *Philosophical Disputes in the Social Sciences* (Brighton: Harvester) pp.127–39.

Aquinas, St. Thomas (1969) *Summa Theologiae* (1265/73) vol. 16 (London: Blackfriars).

Ardrey, R. (1977) *The Hunting Hypothesis* (Glasgow: Fontana).

Arendt, H. (1958) *The Human Condition* (Chicago: University of Chicago Press).

Aristotle, (1910) *On Rhetoric*, trans. T. Buckley (London: George Bell).

Aristotle (1946) *The Politics*, trans. E. Barker (Oxford: Clarendon Press).

Aristotle (1952) *The Eudemian Ethics*, trans. H. Rackham (London: Heinemann Loeb Library).

Aristotle (1967) 'On the Soul' (De Anima), trans. W. Hett, in A. Edel (ed.), *Aristotle Selections* (New York: Dell).

Aristotle (1976) *The Nicomachean Ethics*, trans. J. Thomson and H. Tredennick (Harmondsworth: Penguin).

Augustine, St. (1945) *The City of God* (426), trans. J. Healy (London: Everyman Library).

Aurelius, M. (1961) 'To Himself', in M. Hadas (ed.), *Essential Works of Stoicism* (New York: Bantam) pp.105–205.

Bachrach, P. (1969) *The Theory of Democratic Elitism* (London: University of London Press).

Bachrach, P. (1975) 'Interests, Participation and Democratic Theory', in J. Pennock and J. Chapman (eds), *Participation in Politics* (New York: Lieber-Atherton) pp.39–55.

Bacon, F. (1853) *Novum Organum* (1620) (London: Bohn).

Bagehot, W. (nd.) *Physics and Politics* (London: Kegan Paul).

Baldry, H. C. (1961) *The Unity of Mankind in Greek Thought* (Cambridge: Cambridge University Press).

Bambrough, R. (1975) 'Essay on Man', in R. S. Peters (ed.), *Nature and Conduct* (London: Macmillan) pp.1–13.

145

Barash, D. (1977) *Sociobiology and Behaviour* (New York: Elsevier).
Barash, D. (1980) *Sociobiology: The Whisperings Within* (London: Souvenir).
Barber, B. (1975) 'Justifying Justice', in N. Daniels (ed.), *Reading Rawls* (Oxford: Blackwell) pp.292–318.
Barnes, B. and Bloor, D. (1982) 'Relativism, Rationalism and the Sociology of Knowledge', in M. Hollis and S. Lukes (eds), *Rationality and Relativism* (Oxford: Blackwell) pp.21–47.
Barrett, W. (1962) *Irrational Man: A Study in Existential Philosophy* (New York: Doubleday).
Barry, B. (1973) *The Liberal Theory of Justice* (Oxford: Clarendon Press).
Becker, C. (1942) *The Declaration of Independence: A Study in the History of Political Ideas* (New York: Vintage).
Beckwith, J. (1981) 'The Political Uses of Sociobiology in the United States and Europe', *The Philosophical Forum*, vol. 13, pp.311–22.
Benedict, R. (1968) *Patterns of Culture* (London: Routledge).
Benthall, J. (ed.) (1973) *The Limits of Human Nature* (London: Allen Lane).
Bentham, J. (1859) 'Of the Influence of Time and Place in Matters of Legislation', in *Works*, vol. 1, (Edinburgh: Tait).
Bentham, J. (1948) *Introduction to the Principles of Morals and Legislation* (1789) (Oxford: Blackwell).
Berger, P. and Luckmann, T. (1966) *The Social Construction of Reality* (Harmondsworth: Penguin).
Berghe, P. van der (1978) 'Bridging the Paradigms: Biology and the Social Sciences', in M. Gregory *et al.* (eds), *Sociobiology and Human Nature* (San Francisco: Jossey Bass) pp.33–52.
Berlin, I. (1962) 'Does Political Theory still exist?', in P. Laslett and W. Runciman (eds), *Philosophy, Politics and Society* Second Series (Oxford: Blackwell) pp.1–33.
Berlin, I. (1969) *Four Essays on Liberty* (London: Oxford University Press).
Berlin, I. (1981) *Against the Current* (Oxford: Oxford University Press).
Berry, C. J. (1977) 'From Hume to Hegel: the case of the Social Contract', in *Journal of the History of Ideas*, vol. 38, no. 4, pp.691–703.
Berry, C. J. (1981) 'Nations and Norms', in *The Review of Politics*, vol. 43, no. 1, pp.75–87.
Berry, C. J. (1982) *Hume, Hegel and Human Nature* (The Hague: Martinus Nijhoff).
Berry, C. J. (1983) 'Conservatism and Human Nature', in I. Forbes and S. Smith (eds) *Politics and Human Nature* (London: Frances Pinter) pp.53–67.
Bloch, M. (1977) 'The Past and the Present in the Present', in *Man (New Series)*, vol. 12, pp.278–92.
Boucher, J. D. (1979) 'Culture and Emotion', in A. J. Marsella *et al.*, *Perspectives on Cross-Cultural Psychology* (New York: Academic Press) pp.159–78.

Bowlby, J. (1953) *Child Care and the Growth of Love* (Harmondsworth: Penguin).
Breuer, G. (1982) *Sociobiology and the Human Dimension* (Cambridge: Cambridge University Press).
Burke, E. (1882) 'Reflections on the Revolution in France' (1790), in *Works*, vol. 2 (London: Bohn).
Calvin, J. (1953) *Institutes of the Christian Religion* (1559), trans. H. Beveridge (London: James Clark).
Casey, J. (1973) 'Human Virtue and Human Nature', in J. Benthall (ed.), *The Limits of Human Nature* (London: Allen Lane) pp.74–91.
Cassirer, E. (1944) *An Essay on Man* (New Haven, Conn.: Yale University Press).
Cassirer, E. (1953) *The Philosophy of Symbolic Forms*, trans. R. Mannheim (New Haven, Conn.: Yale University Press).
Chapman, J. W. (1977) 'Toward a general theory of Human Nature and Dynamics', in J. Pennock and J. Chapman (eds) *Human Nature in Politics* (New York: New York University Press), pp.297–319.
Chapman, J. W. (1980) 'Justice, Freedom and Property', in J. Pennock and J. Chapman (eds), *Property* (New York: New York University Press) pp.289–324.
Chase, S. (1950) *The Proper Study of Mankind* (London: Phoenix House).
Cicero (1929) *On the Commonwealth* (51BC) trans. G. Sabine and S. Smith (Indianapolis: Bobbs-Merrill).
Clark, S. (1975) *Aristotle's Man* (Oxford: Clarendon Press).
Colinvaux, P. (1983) *The Fates of Nations: A Biological Theory of History* (Harmondsworth: Penguin).
Colmer, J. (1959) *Coleridge: Critic of Society* (Oxford: Clarendon Press).
Condorcet, M. (1933) *Esquisse d'un Tableau Historique des Progrès de l'Esprit Humain* (1795) (Paris: Boivin).
Connolly, W. (1974) *Terms of Discourse* (Lexington, Mass.: D. C. Heath).
Corning, P. A. (1970–71) 'The Biological Bases of Behavior and some implications for Political Science', *World Politics*, vol. 23, pp.321–70.
Corning, P. A. (1977) 'Human Nature Redivivus', in J. Pennock and J. Chapman (eds) *Human Nature in Politics* (New York: New York University Press), pp.19–68.
Cottingham, J. (1983) 'Neo-Naturalism and its Pitfalls', *Philosophy*, vol. 58, no. 4, pp.455–70.
Crocker, L. (1959) *An Age of Crisis: Man and World in Eighteenth Century French Thought* (Baltimore: Johns Hopkins University Press).
Dahl, R. A. (1956) *Preface to Democratic Theory* (Chicago: University of Chicago Press).
Dahl, R. A. (1970a) *Modern Political Analysis*, Second Edition, (Englewood Cliffs, N.J.: Prentice-Hall).
Dahl, R. A. (1970b) *After the Revolution* (New Haven: Yale University Press).
Darlington, C. D. (1968) *The Evolution of Man and Society* (New York: Simon & Schuster).

Darlington, C. D. (1978) *Little Universe of Man* (London: Allen & Unwin).
Davidson, D. (1984) 'On the very idea of a Conceptual Scheme', in his *Inquiries into Truth and Interpretation* (Oxford: Clarendon Press) pp.183–98.
Davies, J. C. (1963) *Human Nature in Politics* (New York: Wiley).
Davies, J. C. (1977) 'The Priority of Human Needs and the stages of Political Development', in J. Pennock and J. Chapman (eds) *Human Nature in Politics* (New York: New York University Press) pp.157–96.
Davies, J. K. (1978) *Democracy and Classical Greece* (Glasgow: Fontana).
Dawkins, R. (1978) *The Selfish Gene* (London: Paladin).
Dobzhansky, T. (1962) *Mankind Evolving* (New Haven: Yale University Press).
Douglas, M. (1975) *Implicit Meanings: Essays in Anthropology* (London: Routledge & Kegan Paul).
Dubos, R. (1973) *So Human an Animal* (London: Abacus).
Duncan, G. (1983) 'Political Theory and Human Nature', in I. Forbes and S. Smith (eds), *Politics and Human Nature* (London: Frances Pinter) pp.5–19.
Edelman, M. (1971) *Politics as Symbolic Action* (Chicago: Markham).
Eibl-Eibesfeldt, I. (1971) *Love and Hate*, trans. G. Strachan (New York: Holt, Rinehart & Winston).
Eibl-Eibesfeldt, I. (1979) *The Biology of Peace and War*, trans. E. Mosbacher (New York: Viking).
Entrèves, A. P. d' (1951) *Natural Law* (London: Hutchinson).
Epictetus (n.d.) *The Discourses*, trans. G. Long (New York: A. L. Burt).
Eysenck, H. (1975) *The Inequality of Man* (Glasgow: Fontana).
Farb, P. (1978) *Humankind* (London: Paladin).
Fay, B. (1975) *Social Theory and Political Practice* (London: Allen & Unwin).
Fichte, J. G. (1968) *Address to the German Nation* (1808) (New York: Harper Row).
Filmer, R. (1949) *Patriarcha (1680) and other Political Works*, P. Laslett (ed.) (Oxford: Blackwell).
Finnis, J. (1980) *Natural Law and Natural Rights* (Oxford: Clarendon Press).
Flohr, H. and Tönnesmann, W. (eds) (1983) *Politik und Biologie* (Berlin: P. Parey).
Foot, P. (ed.) (1967) *Theories of Ethics* (London: Oxford University Press).
Foot, P. (1978) *Virtues and Vices* (Oxford: Blackwell).
Forbes, I. and Smith, S. (eds) (1983) *Politics and Human Nature* (London: Frances Pinter).
Foucault, M. (1970) *The Order of Things* (London: Tavistock).
Fourier, C. (1971) *The Harmonian Man: Selected Writings*, trans. S. Hanson (Garden City, N.Y.: Anchor).
Freud, S. (1960) *Totem and Taboo*, trans. J. Strachey (London: Routledge & Kegan Paul).

Freud, S. (1964) *The Future of an Illusion*, trans. W. Robson-Scott (Garden City, N.Y.: Anchor).
Fromm, E. and Xirau, R. (eds) (1968) *The Nature of Man* (New York: Macmillan).
Gaus, G. F. (1982) *The Modern Liberal Theory of Man* (London: Croom Helm).
Geertz, C. (1972) *The Interpretation of Cultures* (New York: Basic Books).
Geras, N. (1983) *Marx and Human Nature* (London: Verso Books).
Godwin, W. (1976) *Enquiry Concerning Political Justice* (1798) (Harmondsworth: Penguin).
Gould, C. (1973) 'The Woman Question', *The Philosophical Forum*, vol. 5, no. 1, pp.5–44.
Gray, J. (1978) 'Social Contract, Community and Ideology', in P. Birnbaum, G. Parry and J. Lively (eds) *Democracy, Consensus and Social Contract* (London: Sage) pp.225–43.
Gregory, M. *et al.* (eds) (1978) *Sociobiology and Human Nature* (San Francisco: Jossey-Bass).
Grotius, H. (1957) *Prolegomena to the Laws of War and Peace* (1620), trans. F. Kelsey (Indianapolis: Bobbs-Merrill).
Gunnell, J. G. (1968) *Political Philosophy and Time* (Middletown, Conn.: Wesleyan University Press).
Gunnell, J. G. (1975) *Philosophy, Science and Political Inquiry* (Morristown, N.J.: General Learning Press).
Habermas, J. (1971) *Toward a Rational Society*, trans. J. Shapiro (London: Heinemann).
Habermas, J. (1972) *Knowledge and Human Interests*, trans. J. Shapiro (London: Heinemann).
Hampshire, S. (1962) *Spinoza* (Harmondsworth: Penguin).
Hampshire, S. (1965) *Thought and Action* (London: Chatto & Windus).
Hampshire, S. (1972) 'Fallacies in Moral Philosophy', in his *Freedom of Mind and other Essays* (Oxford: Clarendon Press) pp.42–63.
Hardie, W. F. R. (1968) *Aristotle's Ethical Theory* (Oxford: Clarendon Press).
Hare, R. M. (1961) *The Language of Morals* (Oxford: Oxford University Press).
Hare, R. M. (1963) *Freedom and Reason* (Oxford: Oxford University Press).
Hart, H. L. A. (1961) *The Concept of Law* (Oxford: Clarendon Press).
Hartley, D. (1810) *Observations on Man*, Fifth Edition (London).
Hegel, G. W. F. (1892) *The Logic of Hegel* (1827–30), trans. W. Wallace (Oxford: Clarendon Press).
Hegel, G. W. F. (1942) *The Philosophy of Right* (1821), trans. T. M. Knox (Oxford: Clarendon Press).
Hegel, G. W. F. (1970) *On Art, Religion and Philosophy*, J. G. Gray (ed.) (New York: Harper Row).
Hegel, G. W. F. (1975) *Lectures on the Philosophy of World History* (1830), trans. H. Nisbet (Cambridge: Cambridge University Press).
Heller, A. (1978) *Renaissance Man*, trans. R. Allen (London: Routledge & Kegan Paul).

Herder, G. W. (1891) 'Reise journal 1767', in *Sämtliche Werke*, ed. B. Suphan vol. 4 (Berlin).

Herder, G. W. (1968) *Reflections on the Philosophy of the History of Mankind* (1784) (Chicago: University of Chicago Press).

Herder, G. W. (1969) *On Social and Political Culture*, F. Barnard (ed.) (Cambridge: Cambridge University Press).

Hesse, M. (1981) *Revolutions and Reconstructions in the Philosophy of Science* (Brighton: Harvester).

Hobbes, T. (1840) 'A Dialogue between a philosopher and a student of the Common Laws of England', in *Works*, vol. 6 (London: Bohn).

Hobbes, T. (1914) *Leviathan* (1651) (London: Everyman Library).

Hollis, M. and Lukes. S. (eds) (1982) *Rationality and Relativism* (Oxford: Blackwell).

Hollis, M. (1970a) 'The Limits of Irrationality', in B. Wilson (ed.), *Rationality*, (New York: Harper & Row) pp.214–20.

Hollis, M. (1970b) 'Reason and Ritual', in B. Wilson (ed.), *Rationality* (New York: Harper Row) pp.221–39.

Hollis, M. (1977) *Models of Man* (Cambridge: Cambridge University Press).

Hollis, M. (1979) 'The Epistemological Unity of Mankind', in S. C. Brown (ed.), *Philosophical Disputes in the Social Sciences* (Brighton: Harvester), pp.225–32.

Holmstrom, N. (1982) 'Do Women Have a Distinct Nature?', *The Philosophical Forum*, vol. 14, pp.25–42.

Holmstrom, N. (1984) 'A Marxist Theory of Women's Nature', *Ethics*, vol. 94, pp.456–73.

Horton, R. (1979) 'Material-Object Language and Theoretical Language: Towards a Strawsonian Sociology of Thought', in S. C. Brown (ed.), *Philosophical Disputes in the Social Sciences* (Brighton: Harvester), pp.197–224.

Hume, D. (1888) *A Treatise of Human Nature* (1739–40) (Oxford: Clarendon Press).

Hume, D. (1894) *The History of England* (1786) (Manchester: George Routledge).

Hume, D. (1955) *An Inquiry concerning Human Understanding* (1748) (Indianapolis: Bobbs-Merrill).

Hume, D. (1963) 'Of the Origin of Government' (1777), in *Essays* (Oxford: Oxford University Press) pp.35–9.

Jaggar, A. (1983) *Feminist Politics and Human Nature* (Brighton: Harvester).

Kluckhohn, C. (1953) 'Universal Categories of Culture', in A. Kroeber (ed.), *Anthropology Today*, (Chicago: University of Chicago Press) pp.507–23.

Knutson, J. N. (1972) *The Human Basis of the Polity* (Chicago: Aldine-Atherton).

Kovesi, J. (1967) *Moral Notions* (London: Routledge & Kegan Paul).

Laertius, D. (1961) 'Life of Zeno', in M. Hadas (ed.) *Essential Works of Stoicism* (New York: Bantam) pp.3–47.

Larrain, J. (1979) *The Concept of Ideology* (London: Hutchinson).
Lévi-Strauss, C. (1966) *The Savage Mind* (London: Weidenfeld & Nicolson).
Lévi-Strauss, C. (1968) *Structural Anthropology*, trans. C. Jacobson and B. Scheopf (London: Allen Lane).
Linton, R. (ed.) (1945) *The Science of Man in the World Crisis* (New York: Columbia University Press).
Locke, J. (1948) *A Letter Concerning Toleration* (1689) (Oxford: Blackwell).
Locke, J. (1965) *Two Treatises of Government* (1690) (New York: Mentor).
Lonner, W. J. (1980) 'The search for Psychological Universals', in H. Triandis and W. Lambert (eds), *Handbook of Cross-Cultural Psychology* vol. 1, (Boston: Allyn & Bacon), pp.143–204.
Lopreato, J. (1984) *Human Nature and Biocultural Evolution* (Boston: Allen & Unwin).
Lorenz, K. (1966) *On Aggression*, trans. M. Latzke (London: Methuen).
Lukes, S. (1973) 'The Social Determination of Truth', in R. Horton and R. Finnegan (eds), *Modes of Thought*, (London: Faber) pp.230–48.
MacIntyre, A. (1967) *A Short History of Ethics* (London: Routledge & Kegan Paul).
MacIntyre, A. (1981) *After Virtue* (London: Duckworth).
Mackenzie, W. J. M. (1978) *Biological Ideas in Politics* (Harmondsworth: Penguin).
Macpherson, C. B. (1973) *Democratic Theory: Essays in Retrieval* (Oxford: Clarendon Press).
Macquarrie, J. (1982) *In Search of Humanity* (London: SCM).
McShea, R. J. (1978) 'Human Nature Theory and Political Practice', *American Journal of Political Science*, vol. 22, pp.656–77.
Maistre, J. de (1965) *Works*, ed. and trans. J. Lively (London: Allen & Unwin).
Malinowski, B. (1960) *A Scientific Theory of Culture* (New York: Oxford University Press).
Malson, L. (1972) *Wolf Children*, trans. E. Fawcett (London: New Left Books).
Marx, K. (n.d.) *The Poverty of Philosophy* (1847) (London: Martin Lawrence).
Marx, K. (1967) *Capital* (1867), trans. S. Moore and E. Aveling (New York: New World).
Marx, K. (1973) *Grundrisse* (1857) trans. M. Nicolaus (Harmondsworth: Penguin).
Marx, K. (1975) *Early Writings* (1843/4) trans. G. Benton (Harmondsworth: Penguin).
Marx, K. (1977) 'Eighteenth Brumaire of Louis Bonaparte' (1852), in *Selected Writings*, ed. D. McLellan (Oxford: Oxford University Press).
Maslow, A. (1943) 'A Theory of Human Motivation', *Psychological Review*, vol. 50, pp.370–96.

Meacher, M. (1977) 'The Socialist Alternative', in K. Coates and F. Singleton (eds), *The Just Society* (Nottingham: Spokesman Books), pp.135–48.

Midgley, M. (1978) *Beast and Man* (Brighton: Harvester).

Midgley, M. (1980) 'The Absence of a Gap between Facts and Values', *Proceedings of the Aristotelian Society* vol. 54, pp.207–23.

Mill, J. (1955) *An Essay on Government* (1820) (Indianapolis: Bobbs-Merrill).

Mill, J. S. (1904) 'Nature' (1874) in his *Three Essays on Religion* (London: Watts).

Mill, J. S. (1972) *Utilitarianism* (1863) (London: Everyman Library).

Monro, D. H. (1967) *Empiricism and Ethics* (Cambridge: Cambridge University Press).

Monro, D. J. (1969) *The Concept of Man in Early China* (Stanford: Stanford University Press).

Montague, A. (ed.) (1980) *Sociobiology Examined* (New York: Oxford University Press).

Moore, G. E. (1962) *Principia Ethica* (1903) (Cambridge: Cambridge University Press).

Murdock, G. P. (1945) 'The Common Denominators of Cultures', in R. Linton (ed.), *The Science of Man in the World Crisis* (New York: Columbia University Press) pp.123–42.

Murdock, G. P. (1957) 'World Ethnographic Sample', *American Anthropologist*, vol. 59, pp.664–87.

Myres, J. L. (1927) *The Political Ideas of the Greeks* (London: E. Arnold).

Nietzsche, F. (1907) *Beyond God and Evil* (1886) trans. H. Zimmern (Edinburgh: T. Foulis).

Nietzsche, F. (1933) *Thus Spake Zarathustra* (1883–91) trans. A. Tille (London: Everyman Library).

Nietzsche, F. (1968a) *Twilight of the Idols* (1889) trans. R. Hollingdale (Harmondsworth: Penguin).

Nietzsche, F. (1968b) *The Will to Power* (1884/8) trans. M. Kaufmann and R. Hollingdale (New York: Vintage).

Nott, K. (1970) *Philosophy and Human Nature* (London: Hodder & Stoughton).

Nozick, R. (1974) *Anarchy, State and Utopia* (Oxford: Blackwell).

Oakeshott, M. (1975) *On Human Conduct* (Oxford: Clarendon Press).

Oppenheim, F. (1961) *The Dimensions of Freedom* (New York: St Martins).

Oppenheim, F. (1973) ' "Facts" and "Values" in Politics. Are they Separable?', *Political Theory*, vol. 1, no. 1, pp.54–68.

Owen, R. (1970) *A New View of Society* (1813/4) (Harmondsworth: Penguin).

Paine, T. (1948) 'The Rights of Man' (1791/2), in *Selected Writings*, N. Gangulee (ed.) (London: Nicholson & Watson).

Parekh, B. (1972) 'Liberalism and Morality', in B. Parekh and R. Berki (eds), *The Morality of Politics* (London: Allen & Unwin) pp.81–98.

Parekh, B. (1982) *Contemporary Political Thinkers* (Oxford: Martin Robertson).
Parfit, D. (1984) *Reasons and Persons* (Oxford: Clarendon Press).
Pateman, C. (1970) *Participation and Democratic Theory* (Cambridge: Cambridge University Press).
Pedersen, P. (1979) 'Non-Western Psychology: The Search for Alternatives', in A. J. Marsella *et al. Perspectives on Cross-Cultural Psychology* (New York: Academic Press) pp.77–98.
Pennock, J. and Chapman, J. (eds) (1977) *Human Nature in Politics* (New York: New York University Press).
Plamenatz, J. (1971) *Ideology* (London: Macmillan).
Plato (1955) *The Republic*, trans. H. D. P. Lee (Harmondsworth: Penguin).
Platt, J. R. (ed.) (1965) *New Views of the Nature of Man* (Chicago: University of Chicago Press).
Popper, K. (1968) *Conjectures and Refutations* (New York: Harper Row).
Putnam, H. (1981) *Reason, Truth and History* (Cambridge: Cambridge University Press).
Quinton, A. (1967) 'Editorial Introduction', in his *Political Philosophy* (London: Oxford University Press) pp.1–18.
Quinton, A. (1975) 'Has Man an Essence?', in R. S. Peters (ed.), *Nature and Conduct* (London: Macmillan), pp.13–35.
Raju, P. T. (1960) 'The Indian Concept of Man', in S. Radhakrishnan and P. Raju (eds) *The Concept of Man* (London: Allen & Unwin), pp.206–305.
Rawls, J. (1972) *A Theory of Justice* (London: Oxford University Press).
Rist, J. M. (1969) *Stoic Philosophy* (Cambridge: Cambridge University Press).
Rorty, R. (1980) *Philosophy and the Mirror of Nature* (Oxford: Blackwell).
Rorty, R. (1982) *Consequences of Pragmatism* (Brighton: Harvester).
Rose, S. (1980) ' "It's only Human Nature": The Sociobiologists' Fairyland', in A. Montague (ed.), *Sociobiology Examined* (New York: Oxford University Press), pp.158–70.
Rose, S., Kamin, L. and Lewontin, R. (1984) *Not in our Genes: Biology, Ideology and Human Nature* (Harmondsworth: Penguin).
Rothblatt, B. (ed.) (1968) *Changing Perspectives on Man* (Chicago: University of Chicago Press).
Rousseau, J. J. (1962) *Discours sur l'Origine de l'Inégalité parmi les Hommes* (1755) (Paris: Garnier).
Ryan, A. (1973) 'The Nature of Human Nature in Hobbes and Rousseau', in J. Benthall (ed.), *The Limits of Human Nature* (London: Allen Lane) pp.3–19.
Sahlins, M. (1977) *The Use and Abuse of Biology* (London: Tavistock).
Sartre, J.-P. (1965) *Nausea* (1936), trans. R. Baldick (Harmondsworth: Penguin).
Sartre, J.-P. (1966) *Being and Nothingness* (1943), trans. H. Barnes (New York: Washington Square Press).

Sartre, J.-P. (1973) *Existentialism and Humanism* (1946), trans. P. Mairet (London: Eyre Methuen).

Sayers, J. (1982) *Biological Politics* (London: Tavistock).

Schilcher, F. von and Tennant, N. (1983) *Philosophy, Evolution and Human Nature* (London: Routledge & Kegan Paul).

Schubert, G. (1976) 'Politics as a Life Science', in A. Somit (ed.), *Biology and Politics* (The Hague: Mouton) pp.155–95.

Schumpeter, J. (1950) *Capitalism, Socialism and Democracy* (London: Allen & Unwin).

Schwartz, D. (1976) 'Somatic States and Political Behavior', in A. Somit (ed.), *Biology and Politics* (The Hague: Mouton) pp.15–44.

Seneca, L. A. (1961) 'On Tranquility', in M. Hadas (ed.), *Essential Works of Stoicism* (New York: Bantam) pp.55–81.

Seneca, L. A. (1969) *Letters from a Stoic*, trans. R. Campbell (Harmondsworth: Penguin).

Shelley, P. B. (1970) 'A Defence of Poetry' (1821), in *Political Writings*, R. Duerksen (ed.) (New York: Appleton-Century-Crofts).

Singer, P. (1981) *The Expanding Circle* (Oxford: Clarendon Press).

Skillen, A. (1977) *Ruling Illusions* (Brighton: Harvester).

Skinner, B. F. (1973) *Beyond Freedom and Dignity* (Harmondsworth: Penguin).

Skinner, B. F. (1974) *About Behaviorism* (New York: Knopf).

Skinner, Q. (1978) *The Foundations of Modern Political Thought* (Cambridge: Cambridge University Press).

Smith, A. (1976) *An Inquiry into the Nature and Causes of the Wealth of Nations* (1776) (Oxford: Clarendon Press).

Somit, A. (ed.) (1976) *Biology and Politics* (The Hague: Mouton).

Spinoza, B. (n.d.) *A Political Treatise*, trans. R. Elwes (London: Routledge).

Springborg, P. (1981) *The Problem of Human Needs and the Critique of Civilisation* (London: Allen & Unwin).

Steiner, G. (1975) *After Babel* (London: Oxford University Press).

Stevenson, L. (1974) *Seven Theories of Human Nature* (Oxford: Clarendon Press).

Stevenson, L. (ed.) (1981) *The Study of Human Nature* (New York: Oxford University Press).

Symons, D. (1979) *The Evolution of Human Sexuality* (New York: Oxford University Press).

Talmon, J. L. (1970) *The Origins of Totalitarian Democracy* (London: Sphere Books).

Taylor, C. (1973) 'Neutrality in Political Science', in A. Ryan (ed.), *The Philosophy of Social Explanation* (London: Oxford University Press) pp.139–70.

Thorpe, W. H. (1974) *Animal Nature and Human Nature* (London: Methuen).

Trigg, R. (1980) *Reality at Risk* (Brighton: Harvester).

Trigg, R. (1982) *The Shaping of Man: Philosophical Aspects of Sociobiology* (Oxford: Blackwell).

Tuck, R. (1979) *Natural Rights Theories* (Cambridge: Cambridge University Press).

Tudor, H. (1972) *Political Myth* (London: Macmillan).

Voltaire, F. M. A. (1956) 'Letter to Frederick of Prussia, October 1737', in *Candide and other writings*, H. M. Block (ed.) (New York: Modern Library).

Waddington, C. H. (1960) *The Ethical Animal* (London: Allen & Unwin).

Wallace, G. and Walker, A. (eds) (1970) *The Defence of Morality* (London: Methuen).

Wallas, G. (1924) *Human Nature in Politics*, Third Edition (London: Constable).

Walsh, W. H. (1975) 'The Constancy of Human Nature', in H. D. Lewis (ed.), *Contemporary British Philosophy* (London: Allen & Unwin) pp.274–90.

Warnock, G. (1967) *Contemporary Moral Philosophy* (London: Macmillan).

Whorf, B. L. (1956) *Language, Thought and Reality*, J. B. Carroll (ed.) (Cambridge, Mass.: MIT Press).

Williams, B. (1972) *Morality: An Introduction to Ethics* (Cambridge: Cambridge University Press).

Wilson, B. (ed.) (1970) *Rationality* (New York: Harper & Row).

Wilson, E. O. (1978) *On Human Nature* (Cambridge, Mass.: Harvard University Press).

Wilson, E. O. and Lumsden, C. J. (1981) *Genes, Mind and Culture* (Cambridge: Mass.: Harvard University Press).

Winch, P. (1970) 'Understanding a Primitive Society', in B. Wilson (ed.) *Rationality* (New York: Harper Row) pp.78–111.

Winch, P. (1971) 'Human Nature', in G. Vesey (ed.) *The Proper Study* (London: Macmillan) pp.1–13.

Wolin, S. (1972) 'Political Theory as a Vocation', in M. Fleisher (ed.), *Machiavelli and the Nature of Political Thought* (New York: Atheneum) pp.23–75.

Yankelovich, D. (1973) 'The Idea of Human Nature', *Social Research*, vol. 40, no. 3, pp.407–28.

Young, R. (1971) 'Evolutionary Biology and Ideology: Then and Now', *Science Studies*, vol. 1, pp.177–206.

Young, R. (1973a) 'The Human Limits of Nature', in *The Limits of Human Nature*, ed. J. Benthall (London: Allen Lane) pp.235–74.

Young, R. (1973b) 'The Historiographic and Ideological Context of the Nineteenth Century Debate of Man's Place in Nature', in M. Teich and R. Young (eds), *Changing Perspectives in the History of Science* (London: Heinemann) pp.344–438.

Index